LITERARY BLASPHEMIES

OTHER BOOKS BY ERNEST BOYD

IRELAND'S LITERARY RENAISSANCE

THE CONTEMPORARY DRAMA OF IRELAND

STUDIES FROM TEN LITERATURES

GUY DE MAUPASSANT: A BIOGRAPHICAL STUDY

LITERARY BLASPHEMIES
BY
ERNEST BOYD

GREENWOOD PRESS, PUBLISHERS
NEW YORK

Copyright © 1927 by Ernest Boyd

Reprinted by permission
of Harper and Brothers, Publishers

First Greenwood Reprinting 1969

Library of Congress Catalogue Card Number 76-90472

SBN 8371-2516-2

PRINTED IN UNITED STATES OF AMERICA

TO
THOMAS BEER
FOR HIS MORE GRACEFUL
BLASPHEMIES

CONTENTS

I	AN ADDRESS TO THE INDIGNANT READER	3
II	WILLIAM SHAKESPEARE	16
III	JOHN MILTON	43
IV	JONATHAN SWIFT	74
V	LORD BYRON	106
VI	CHARLES DICKENS	136
VII	EDGAR ALLAN POE	163
VIII	WALT WHITMAN	186
IX	HENRY JAMES	213
X	THOMAS HARDY	227
XI	EPILOGUE	256

LITERARY BLASPHEMIES

Chapter One

AN ADDRESS TO
THE INDIGNANT READER

THE reception accorded to certain chapters of this book which were published while the work was in progress makes it necessary to explain what otherwise might be deducible from the title. These essays do not aim at being exhaustive or impartial, nor at proving that the writers discussed are worthless. Most of the classics have survived frequent and harsher criticism, so that it is quite unnecessary to remind me that Shakespeare will be remembered long after I am forgotten. In fact, if some degree of immortality did not attach to them, I should not have discussed them, for a similar examination of contemporary reputations would be pointless, since current criticism deals with the living precisely as I have tried to deal with the dead.

What I have attempted is something easier, perhaps, to define than to execute. I have assumed that an adult reader, familiar with modern literature and modern ideas, has heretofore been able to ignore the classics and is vaguely aware that professors speak of them with respect, but that the average person does them reverence very much as the average Christian reveres Christ. That is to say, neither practices what he preaches. It is much easier to do lip service to the beauties of Milton and Shakespeare while reading *Gentlemen Prefer Blondes,* or Zane Grey, for pleasure, than to confess that one finds Wild West fiction as unendurable as many works of the immortal dead, and to say so frankly. It is my belief that a widespread and honest effort to reconcile theory and practice would be as fatal to classical literature as to orthodox Christianity. Many reputations survive in the class-room as many Christian virtues survive only in church. Furthermore, just as there are people who genuinely enjoy "Paradise Lost" and prefer it to the latest novel, so there have been rare individuals who tried to live according to the teaching of Christ. Literature has its Tolstoys no less than religion. But in neither case is there any excuse for crediting the majority with virtues which they manifestly do not possess.

I have tried to reread a group of English and American classical authors from the point of view of a man who is entirely unimpressed or unconvinced by the conventional attitude adopted towards established reputations, who brings to them

TO THE INDIGNANT READER

a fresh mind, colored only by such tastes, prejudices, and weaknesses as are given free play in the discussion of contemporaries. The artificiality of most criticism of the classics is nowhere more obvious than in its careful avoidance of all comment of an avowedly personal and human character. There is a sort of game of critical chess; certain variations of opening and strategy are permissible, but every statement follows a gambit predetermined by academic precedents, and the end is as much a foregone conclusion as a checkmate or a stalemate. Novelty is possible only if new documents have been discovered, and then it is to scholarship rather than to pure criticism that the reader is indebted.

Many eminent critics at the present time do not hesitate to admit that they admire Joseph Conrad but are unmoved by George Moore, or that they have found their pleasure in Rudyard Kipling marred by his jingoism. Why should not the same latitude be allowed to a reader who, it is assumed, has read Milton and Swift for the first time, ignores or is unaware of the orthodox view of them, and is as dismayed by the superstitious intolerance of the former as he is attracted by the intellectual honesty of the latter? To answer that Milton and Swift have "stood the test of time," whereas Joseph Conrad and George Moore have yet to prove their immortality, is to beg the question, since the assumption is that they are to be judged by the specific impression they make, not accepted on the strength of previous assertions concerning them. If a thug were to recite the Ten Commandments when called upon to explain himself, a barbarian would naturally be astonished to learn that we regarded this performance as proof of his integrity. He would judge the thug by his deeds, not by his professions . . . and so do we in fact.

The greatest heat in resenting these literary blasphemies, it so happens, has been shown by critics whose tastes in current literature are most incompatible with their zeal on behalf of the classics. It is as difficult to reconcile their unerring preference for the shoddy, ephemeral, and popular books of the moment with their indignation at any criticism of the immortals as it is to reconcile the spectacle of a parson blessing a war with the principles of Christ. That the latter spectacle is not unfamiliar, and that patriotic Christians have defended it, and quoted the Bible for their purpose, does not alter the fact that the thing is incongruous and self-contradictory. If we were not accustomed for the past nineteen hundred and twenty-seven years to this divergence between theory and practice, we should be as prompt

TO THE INDIGNANT READER

to notice it as any pacifist eager to justify his personal unwillingness to fight. There is a lot to be said for wars, and a great deal has been said about the teaching of Christ, but a cynical smile is the only appropriate comment on the attempt to make these twain meet.

There are critics, similarly, whose instinct for what the public wants is surpassed only by their timidity in questioning the merits of the great. Were they ever to champion a neglected work of merit by a contemporary, or to attack some specious work of synthetic genius, they might finally develop heretical views about the great writers of the past. Apparently they find their ready acquiescence in the opinions of the critics who have preceded them a consolation for their present failure to do their critical duty. When a new novel of little worth but great pretensions is selling well, they justify themselves by reminding us that Dickens also sold well. Dickens, indeed, despite the superiority of Thackeray, seems to be the favorite of this type of critic, judging by the amount of resentment which my chapter on him provoked, as witness the following characteristic comment on my statement that no adult of mature taste could read Dickens if he had not acquired the habit as a child:

"No person of mature taste encounters Dickens

for the first time. Persons of taste have had their taste matured by reading him. Men of forty of mature taste have in their childhood read Dickens with delight, in their middle years with enthusiasm, and in their later years will read him with wonder at the miracle of such stupendous genius." There must be several millions of people in this world whose language is not English, but who, nevertheless, have had their taste matured, to whom Dickens is barely a name. I have known many distinguished men and many of mature taste who could not reread him. Between the ages of twelve and fifteen I devoured every line written by Dickens that could be found in print, not merely the usual novels and stories, yet I confess it was a painful operation, helped by skipping many pages, to look through some of his most popular books when writing my chapter on him. That criticism is a typical flight to the safe convention. It ignores not only the whole point of the discussion, namely, the postulate that Dickens is being read for the first time, but it also ignores the existence of the majority of the human race, which has had its taste no more matured by Dickens than by the English Bible.

Another argument in support of Dickens which was widely employed was the demand for his works at the public libraries. In discussing

TO THE INDIGNANT READER

Dickens I have explicitly stated that, unlike many of the other subjects of this book, he is one of the few classics who are independent of academic exegetists, and I have viewed him as a specimen of the kind of author whom the plain people would like to immortalize if left to themselves. The demand for him at the libraries emphasizes the truth of my contention. The fiction most in demand at the public libraries in the United States during the year 1926, according to statistics, coincided almost exactly with the fiction that ranked as best sellers in the book shops. In other words, according to the test invoked by his own champions Dickens appeals to the kind of people who read *Pollyanna*.

The chapter on Milton has caused a great deal of pain. I was reminded that his *Areopagitica* is one of the classic pronouncements in favor of the freedom of the press; likewise that the "Hymn to the Nativity" is a very beautiful piece of immortal poetry. Had I not discussed the former precisely in terms of that claim on its behalf and endeavored to show that it was prompted, not by any zeal for freedom of speech but by the necessities of Milton's own personal dilemma, I might have accepted the suggestion that I did not know the platitudes of literature when I saw them. The presence of the "Hymn to the Nativity" in every handbook and anthology, while it might substantiate the claim as to its beauty, does not convince me that, as was charged, my acquaintance with the writings of Milton is superficial. The personality, life, and writings of Milton were such that, if he were alive today, such comment as mine would be regarded as perfectly legitimate.

Nowadays we should have no hesitation in pointing out that Milton was a psychopathic Puritan. He was an undersized man with the pigmentation of an albino, and as abnormal physically as most infant phenomena are. There is evidence suggesting that his mysterious affection of the eyes was the result of hereditary syphilis. He was cold, egocentric, and inhuman in his relations with his friends and relatives; paranoia is written all over his first divorce tract. Having failed to change the marriage laws of Christendom, and his paroxysm of rage having subsided, Milton saw nothing grotesque in a reconciliation, although he had written three furious fulminations against his wife and was the laughing stock of his contemporaries. He had all the worst traits of the Puritan: an overweening confidence in his own conscience as the arbiter of all conduct; a complete inability to comprehend people and circumstances other than his own; a total lack of all sense of humor; and the most callous indifference to all that is charming and beautiful in life.

TO THE INDIGNANT READER

Even those who admit that Milton's "Paradise Lost" and "Paradise Regained" are seldom read through by the majority of educated people, insist that the man himself was a noble figure and, therefore, entitled to our respect. He is praised as a champion of freedom, despite the fact that as Latin secretary he discharged in the most severe manner the duties of a censor, after having clamored for the abolition of all censorship in *Areopagitica.* His denunciations of monarchy and absolutism did not preclude him from fawning on Cromwell— the Mussolini of his day—and praising Christina of Sweden, an absolute ruler who happened to admire his *Defence of the English People.* In his *Tenure of Kings and Magistrates* it suited his purpose to argue that men were born free and fit to rule themselves. But in *Observations upon the Articles of Peace with the Irish Rebels* he finds it convenient to hold that the Irish are "rightly the vassals of the English." *Of True Religion and the Growth of Popery* is an argument directly in contradiction of his claim for freedom to testify and speak according to his conscience, for it denies that privilege to Catholics. In his *Doctrina Christiana,* this pious Bible Christian indulges in sophistries on the subject of lying and deceit which make Machiavelli sound like a child, and which, in their distortion of Scriptural texts, are a perfect compendium of evangelical hypocrisy. When he wanted a divorce, the Old Testament was his guide; otherwise he declared that the New Testament was the end and fulfillment of the Mosaic law.

Milton, as I have tried to show in my essay on him, survives chiefly because he is the one poet produced by Puritanism. He was not, however, so loyal and enthusiastic a devotee of the cause as is commonly supposed. He came home from the Continent ostensibly to help in the Civil War, but he never bore arms. He found it more discreet to open a school until it became quite safe to come out openly for the Presbyterians. Until the censorship was removed he did not risk a word in their favor, and he refrained from attacking the king until the latter had been executed. Thus he later escaped the punishment visited upon the regicides after the Restoration. Milton's official biographer and panegyrist, Masson, ingenuously states that "he showed himself a complete follower of Oliver, but did not wish to lose Bradshaw's favor in the event of a republican counter-revolution." In other words, he supported Cromwell and kept in the good graces of Cromwell's opponent. If Milton were living at this hour we should say that he was a time-server and mere opportunist; that he was a fanatic and a self-seeking party

TO THE INDIGNANT READER

man. Why, then, is he held up as a martyr to a noble cause, one of England's greatest fighters for intellectual freedom; a saintly poet? Pride and hatred were his governing passions, and if his poetry were read, instead of being taken for granted, the man would be found reflected therein.

In speaking thus of the immortals one is accused of "hero-baiting" and of trying to mislead "demi-literates." Yet, it must be obvious that the demi-literate are more certainly obfuscated by the flow of conventional praise of unread and often unreadable classics. The exaction of tokens of perfunctory respect is not a service to literature, for the modern educated illiterate is merely confirmed in his notion that, save for two or three of the more popular novelists like Dickens, great writers are intended for class-room consumption, and he picks his "great" contemporary authors from the lists of best sellers. By a reverse process, it is misleading to our semi-literate poets of to-day when they find Walt Whitman enveloped in a haze of conventional praise as uncritical and sentimental as the previous attacks upon him as an immoral writer. The admirers of Whitman, curiously enough, who raged so furiously against my criticism of him seemed to be unaware of the position of honor which he holds amongst the practitioners of freak prose and poetry both here and in Europe. They denied his paternity, although his literary offspring are proud of it. My premise is not a theory of mine, but a fact of contemporary literary history, to which there are many enthusiastic witnesses. I am not enthusiastic, and it seems to me relevant to trace the connection between his graceless English and the mutilation of that language which is so common in America that eminent professors are writing books on the subject while . . . warmly defending Whitman, just to show how unacademic and modern they are.

Having never in my life read an author because he was part of a prescribed course, never having studied any literature as a duty, I feel that my attitude is free from the reactions induced by returning to subjects once rendered hateful, or at least compulsory, by pedagogues. I have always reread the classics in exactly the same spirit and for the same motive as first attracted me to them. If I have undergone any revulsion of feeling, the change has been natural; if I have modified my enthusiasm for some authors and discovered a new enthusiasm for others, it is thanks to that fact that I have been able to approach my subject in the manner already defined. Not all of these essays are hostile; none pretends to be exhaustive. But each one is an honest attempt to set down the impressions of a reader who has cleared his mind of

TO THE INDIGNANT READER

current critical cant. I have discussed a group of the foremost writers in English and American literature as freely as if they were contemporaries with reputations still undecided. It will be superfluous, therefore, to assure me that all the best people think them impeccable and infallible.

Chapter Two

WILLIAM SHAKESPEARE

NOTHING but the spread of popular education could put culture so effectively upon the defensive as it has been ever since intellectual illiteracy was substituted for the beautiful old custom of making one's mark. As that education has been essentially literary, it is upon literature that its full effect has made itself felt. Consequently, it is without surprise, if not without embarrassment, that I find myself engaged in this meditation. Is there, I ask myself, any honest reason, apart from the educational superstition of the age, why normally happy men and women should be troubled by the immortal glories of literature? We accept so much on trust that one may well hesitate to complicate life by suggesting the innovation of cultural self-determination. The blessings of intellectual democracy, like those of political democracy, obviously consist in the vast weight of responsibility which is taken from the shoulders of the individual, who, as the phrase goes, "instructs" his representatives to act for him. In return, his representatives act first for him and think afterward.

Literature has its catchwords and abstractions just like politics, and "the instruction" from the people in this case goes back to the instructors in departments of English, to the schoolmasters, to the lecturers, and even to the critics, whence it came. It is so clearly unnecessary to have read Shakespeare in order to talk about him, it is so demonstrably impossible to read him under the conditions usually prescribed by educators, that many people prefer to leave him "marked as read." This risk they would not take with the latest novel in which synthetic gin and petting are mixed in the correct proportions, or with the most elusive psychological murex fished up out of the subconscious by the momentarily most popular exponent of the New Salaciousness. As well suppose that the intelligent voter who stands attentively within earshot of the amplifier recording a politician's speech on the League of Nations is going to prepare himself by studying the principles of deflation, by reading the Peace Treaty or even the Articles of the League itself. It is possible, thanks to the march of progress, to savor the prose of, let us say, Mr. Cabell or Ethel and Floyd Dell without having trembled at Marlowe's equally idiotic but mightier lines.

LITERARY BLASPHEMIES

Almost as happy as the nation that has no history is the author who has no annotator—a state in which the defenceless dead rarely find themselves for long, unless they are worse than dead. Even then they may be resuscitated, like the author whose name is at the head of this chapter, and whom the French, for reasons best known to themselves, always refer to as "poor Will"—perhaps because they have seen him performed by actor-managers, or edited and bowdlerized, with an Introduction and notes, by an English or American professor. Living authors and dead have commentators; some living authors enjoy the dubious honor of scholarly annotation, but the sign manual of classical glory for a work of literature is to live on at the hands of successive annotators. The commentator may be a learned critic or an articulate enthusiast. The annotator is the teacher of literature who gets his notions of style from newspaper editorials but reads Shakespeare for his syntax, for his use of the supernatural and the split infinitive, or for his geography. If he were not a relatively recent acquisition of the human race, modern literatures would be as much the prey of the professional scholar as the literatures of Greece and Rome. Only here and there a few isolated amateurs would survive, who actually read with ease and for pleasure the text that launched a thousand grammarians. The obsolescence of a living author begins from the moment the pedant's ferule is pointed at him with instructive intent. People would probably cease to read at all if current literature were not too vast to be inclosed in college courses, and if almost every author alive today had not been ignored or denounced by his contemporary pundits precisely in the degree of his originality.

The first assurance which the average person suffering from modern education has a right to demand is that the immortal classics are not as depressingly perfect as our pastors and masters have insisted. Do they enjoy the suffrages of the hidebound pedant because they are as dull as he would show them to be? Are they so far superior to the books which he borrows from the circulating library in those secret moments when he needs relaxation? Have they no points in common with those subversive volumes which his daughter tries in vain to save from his indignant innocence? Assuredly not. There is as much heresy in the works which no gentleman's library should be without as in the most recent batik-sided, large-paper, signed, *de luxe* edition of the civilized minority's idol of the moment. There is as much platitudinous wisdom as in a New Thought book or a syndicated editorial. There is nearly as much incoherence and fustian as in the works of these æsthetes who make no compromise with the public taste. But there is something more. Hence my charitable belief that by facing English literature steadily and facing it whole, one may combine the vices of contemporaneity with the virtues of immortality.

Shakespeare in our time plays many parts: he comes in handy at college entertainments; he enables advocates of the theater of to-morrow to experiment beyond even their accustomed limits, and champions of the theater of yesterday (or the day before) to restore to the stage for a few nights the vestiges of a simpler and purer epoch. He is a recurrent malady with actors and actresses who have become stars by less strenuous undertakings, and he enables eminent elocutionists to demonstrate through a half century of virtuous theatrical life in small towns that the noblest achievements of histrionic art are not at all incompatible with a blameless and perfect domesticity. In England he has procured knighthoods for those who knew how to shape his rough-hewn ends to meet the requirements of admirers of "East Lynne." In general, wherever they speak the tongue that Shakespeare spoke, "poor Will" serves divers and exceedingly diverse ends. Societies invoking his name used to read his works—with such deletions as mixed company required—in the provinces before the

WILLIAM SHAKESPEARE

brighter dawn of the movie era; professors edited him; experts on the Elizabethan playhouse gave him a prominence which he never enjoyed in those theaters which they have so meticulously described; Americans proved that he never existed; the Germans simply had him superbly translated, and still insist on performing him as successfully as if he were the author of a bedroom farce. The one thing that has almost never been achieved for him in English is the actual performance of his own work.

Inevitably he is still the greatest ornament of the stage, and even more inevitably he is the supreme glory of English literature. Only races tinged with dolichocephalism—this last of the great plagues—are notoriously blind to his grandeur. The French, in particular, have recorded their convictions of him in terms reminiscent of Dr. Stuart Sherman's appreciations of Theodore Dreiser. Voltaire claimed to have been the first to discover him in France, but he finally declared that the author of "Hamlet" was a "drunken savage." In case this judgment be attributed to professional jealousy (for Voltaire was in the classical drama business himself) and in order that the word of an atheist should not stand alone against the reputation of a great English genius, let the eminently Christian Count Leo Tolstoy be heard: "All

Shakespeare's characters speak a language which is not their own, but Shakespeare's, and always the same; pompous, bombastic and artificial, a language which not only could not have been spoken by the characters in these plays but could never have been spoken anywhere by any human beings." Wherefore the creator of Anna Karenina concluded: "the works of Shakespeare do not satisfy any of the demands of art, and moreover, their tendency is most immoral."

However, it is true that both these worthy men had the common misfortune to be barbarians, in the complete sense of that word; they were not English. What of "this blessed plot; this earth, this realm, this England," this "other Eden, demi-paradise," as William himself confidingly called it? Are the records of British opinion more reassuring? David Hume was so magnanimous as to say of Shakespeare: "His total ignorance of all theatrical art and conduct, however material a defect, yet as it affects the spectator rather than the reader, we can more easily excuse, than that want of taste which often prevails in his productions." Ben Jonson's praise of him is unique amongst contemporary testimony, and against it may be set Robert Greene's: "An upstart clown, beautified with our feathers, that with his tiger's heart wrapt in a player's hide, supposes he is as well able to bombast out a blanke verse as the best of you." Even Dryden, who may claim credit for the earliest effort to rescue Shakespeare from neglect, had his doubts, and felt it his duty to rewrite "The Tempest" for the stage. On the first of March, 1662, Mr. Pepys went to see "Romeo and Juliet," and his diary records: "It is a play of itself the worst ever I heard, and the worse acted that ever I saw these people do." At "A Midsummer Night's Dream" he saw "the most insipid, ridiculous play that ever I saw in my life. I saw, I confess, some good dancing and some handsome women, which was all my pleasure." After two attempts his verdict on "Twelfth Night" was that it was "silly, one of the weakest plays that ever I saw on the stage."

Nearly eighty years passed before "Romeo and Juliet" was again revived in London, and then by David Garrick, the man who was to do most for Shakespeare before he was finally canonized and thrown to the professors. Garrick profited by the prevalent indifference to set a precedent for all subsequent actor-managers worthy of the name. "I have," he wrote, "brought 'Hamlet' forth without the grave diggers' trick and the fencing match," without what he termed "all the rubbish of the fifth act." He also did some repair work on "Romeo and Juliet" in order to improve the fifth act. With the result, as a first-nighter of the period reports, that he "rendered the catastrophe the most affecting in the whole compass of the drama." Evidently fifth acts were Shakespeare's weakest point. Garrick was encouraged by the creation of a Shakespeare Club of earnest ladies who bespoke each week some play by their (now) "immortal poet." Editions of Shakespeare's works began to follow one another, edited by eminent hands— Rowe, Pope, Theobald, Hammer, Warburton, and Johnson. For one hundred years after his death only six editions of his collected plays appeared, but in the next fifty there were twenty-three.

At once this evidence of appreciation caused apprehension; it seemed as if an Englishman of genius were really going to be taken seriously, contrary to the laws of nature, so to speak. Thus the good Mrs. Barbauld, in a letter written in 1776, declared, "I am of your opinion that we idolize Shakespeare rather too much for a Christian country." He was advancing from the stage to the library, with consequences which were to justify this dear lady's fears, but in a sense which she can hardly have anticipated. Very soon "mystical Germans," in Gilbertian phrase, were to arise and call Shakespeare great without qualifications; Huns like Lessing, whose æsthetic necessities knew no law of the dramatic unities, and who, as Coleridge

WILLIAM SHAKESPEARE

says, "proved to all thinking men"—even to Shakespeare's own countrymen—"the true nature of his apparent irregularities." A real turning point was reached almost simultaneously with the bi-centenary of Shakespeare's birth. In the year of grace 1818, Dr. T. Bowdler made his own name immortal by publishing an edition of the works "in which those words and expressions are omitted which cannot with propriety be read aloud in a family." The popularity of readings from Shakespeare, one would have thought, was from that moment assured, if not that of the learned editor's edition.

At this point "poor Will" may be observed in such circumstances as might seem to guarantee his place in the affections of all weak and finite mortals. Inferior persons have emended and patronized him, the ladies have discovered him, and the moralists have denounced and bowdlerized him. In the literary market place to-day one alone of these factors would make an author irresistible. Nevertheless, having parsed him and studied footnotes on him, most of us take the rest for granted. When at intervals the David Garricks and Mrs. Siddonses of the moment clear out some "rubbish" from his plays—and from their theaters, incidentally—and give us one of those hectic Shakespearian revivals, we are happy when fond memory brings a nod of recognition to phrases preserved from our oblivion by constant editorial and oratorical usage. Those who have not enjoyed to the last drop the resources of popular education, who have not been "taught" English literature, are deprived of even that flicker of familiarity with the great. Those who have enjoyed it strive without much difficulty to forget it, and are unmoved when John Masefield and others cry out in their anguish:

There is no theatre in London set apart for the performance of Shakespeare. There is no theatre in London built for the right production of Shakespeare. There are not in the empire enough lovers of Shakespeare, or of the poetical drama, or of poetry, to take the British stage from the hands of ground landlords, and make it again glorious with the vision of the pageant of man. . . . Man's true empire is not in continents or over the sea, but within himself, in his own soul. Here in London, where a worldly empire is controlled, there exists no theatre in which the millions can see that other empire. They pass from one gray street to another gray street, to add up figures, or to swallow patent medicines, with no thought that life has been lived nobly and burningly and knightly, for great ends, and in great passions, as the vision of our great mind declares.

It would seem, then, as if Shakespeare had in him all the elements which should endear him to

WILLIAM SHAKESPEARE

the plain people, and none of the dreary virtues with which the mandarins of literature endow the objects of their jealous idolatry. Shakespeare idolatry, however, is a strange cult; a thoroughly Judaistic æsthetic which says: "Thou shalt have none other gods before me," but at the same time inculcates that Jewish suspicion of image-making to which Mr. Masefield alludes in his meditation upon the capital of the British Empire. Thus a twofold phenomenon is created by this curious religion: one is asked simultaneously to worship Shakespeare and to join in the conspiracy to make him unintelligible, unenjoyable, and inaccessible. To this end it is essential that he shall be annotated more than any other writer in the world, that he shall be hedged about with fictitious virtues, and that he shall never be acted as he wrote. So remarkably has this been achieved that people of a naturally credulous disposition will hardly believe Shakespeare can do anything that their favorites of to-day can do. He can offer humor as healthily elementary as that of the Marx brothers; he can wave the flag—British, it is true—with the effective gusto of Mr. George M. Cohan; he can psychoanalyze as subtly as Marcel Proust. He can portray girls as sweet as any in the pages of Ethel M. Dell and more fascinatingly wild than the flapper heroines of the jazz age. He can combine

LITERARY BLASPHEMIES

James Branch Cabell's all-too-human imagination with the austere beauty of the poetry of Robert Frost. In brief, he is everything that is denounced to-day in the popular objects of his academic champions' wrath, together with all that they have never noticed in living genius and have rarely extracted even from his own works. Shakespeare, in other words, is much more entertaining than his classroom champions indicate, and the reproaches of his more candid friends have this quality in common with St. Augustine's "Confessions"—they "make the reader envy his transgressions" as Byron succinctly put it.

On the one hand he is rendered inhuman by the Bardolators, who resolutely refuse to know anything of his life and ideas because whenever a fact stares them in the face it upsets their conception of him as the incarnation of a syndicated newspaper sermon. On the other hand he is abused by reformers and by exponents of the Higher Illiteracy, who have no use for the humanities in education, who prefer a ton of Freudian theory to an ounce of Shakespearian practice. "What a crew they are," cries one of these indignant Moderns, "these Saturday-to-Monday athletic stockbroker Orlandos, these villains, clowns, drunkards, cowards, intriguers, fighters, lovers, patriots, hypochondriacs, who mistake themselves (and are mistaken

WILLIAM SHAKESPEARE

by the author) for philosophers; princes without any sense of public duty, futile pessimists who imagine they are confronting a barren and unmeaning world when they are only contemplating their own worthlessness. . . . Search for statesmanship, or even citizenship, or any sense of the commonwealth, material and spiritual, and you will not find the making of a decent vestryman or curate in the whole horde. As to faith, hope, courage, conviction, or any of the true heroic qualities, you find nothing but death made sensational, despair made stage-sublime, sex made romantic, and barrenness covered up by sentimentality and the mechanical lilt of blank verse."

Compare that outburst with this: "Each book, with its bewildering mass of detail, is a ferocious argument in behalf of a few brutal generalizations. To the eye cleared of illusions it appears that the ordered life which we call civilization does not exist except on paper. In reality our so-called society is a jungle in which the struggle for existence continues, and must continue, on terms substantially unaltered by legal, moral, or social conventions. The central truth about man is that he is an animal amenable to no law but the law of his own temperament, doing as he desires, subject only to the limitations of his power. The male of the species is characterized by cupidity, pugnacity, and a simian inclination for the other sex. The female is a soft, vain, pleasure-seeking creature, devoted to personal adornment, and quite helplessly susceptible to the flattery of the male."

The one is the comment of an ultra-modern dramatic critic on Shakespeare, the other is an indictment of Theodore Dreiser by an ultra-conservative professor. The American novelist has been made by such indignation as this, but his opponents are chary of applying similar tests to the classics. Yet Carrie Meeber and Jennie Gerhardt, whose weaknesses excite the scorn of Dr. Stuart Sherman, are not of that type which Shakespeare so often described, in language which I prefer to that just quoted:

> . . . Fie, fie upon her!
> There's language in her eye, her cheek, her lip,
> Nay, her foot speaks; her wanton spirit looks out
> At every joint and motive of her body.
> O! these encounterers, so glib of tongue,
> That give a coasting welcome ere it comes,
> And wide unclasp the tables of their thoughts
> To every tickling reader, set them down
> For sluttish spoils of opportunity
> And daughters of the game. . . .

The mandarins who have so keen an eye for the ribaldries and the disconsolate veracities of contemporary fiction evade these issues when presented

WILLIAM SHAKESPEARE

in Shakespeare. William had a low sense of humor which impressed the Dr. Bowdler hereinbefore mentioned, but his successors gulp hastily when they come to such passages and murmur soothing nothings about the coarseness of the age. But they do not explain why Spenser before him, and Bunyan immediately after him, were not infected by the spacious atmosphere of Elizabethan frankness. Mr. Frank Harris, whose autobiography is not permitted to contaminate this simple American civilization, is outraged by the freedom of Shakespeare's "salamanders," those dreadfully free young women, like Helena and Beatrice, whose technic and language are essentially in the tone of our latest flapper fiction. "All's Well that Ends Well" begins at once with a conversation between Helena and Parolles which will remind the American reader of to-day of a studio party in Greenwich Village. What a professor calls "the sacred boldness" of this emancipated and shameless creature is in the latest tradition, which disturbs the guardians of our morals and provides endless occupation for societies that specialize in vice. Like her contemporary type Helena protests

> I am a simple maid; and therein wealthiest
> That I protest I simply am a maid.

But her pursuit of the male is as Dreiserian as her

physiological meditations are authentic Floyd Dell. For all that, there are more eager patrons for *Flaming Youth* and *Janet March* than for "Much Ado about Nothing."

While this side of Shakespeare's works is ignored or explained away, much academic praise is lavished upon his platitudinous "philosophy" and his smug homilies:

> Though I look old, yet I am strong and lusty;
> For in my youth I never did apply
> Hot and rebellious liquors in my blood,
> Nor did not with unbashful forehead woo
> The means of weakness and debility;
> Therefore my age is as a lusty winter,
> Frosty, but kindly.

The suspicion that the "worthy master William Shakespeare" was a middle-class English humbug becomes irresistible on reading such lines as these, which have all the conviction of a politician's endorsement of Prohibition. He even went so far as to complain—in 1600 or thereabouts—that servants were not what they used to be:

> O good old man! how well in thee appears
> The constant service of the antique world,
> When service sweat for duty, not for meed!
> Thou art not for the fashion of these times,
> Where none will sweat but for promotion,

WILLIAM SHAKESPEARE
And having that, do choke their service up
Even with the having: it is not so with thee.

Presumably the working classes had become demoralized, as usual, by high wages in munition factories during the war with Spain.

The quintessential commonplace is found in this typical picture of the wealthy townsman's notion of country life:

> Hath not old custom made this life more sweet
> Than that of painted pomp? Are not these woods
> More free from peril than the envious court?
> Here feel we but the penalty of Adam,
> The seasons' difference; as, the icy fang
> And churlish chiding of the winter's wind,
> Which, when it bites and blows upon my body
> Even till I shrink with cold, I smile and say
> "This is no flattery: these are counsellors
> That feelingly persuade me what I am."
> Sweet are the uses of adversity,
> Which like the toad, ugly and venomous,
> Wears yet a precious jewel in his head;
> And this our life exempt from public haunt,
> Finds tongues in trees, books in the running brooks,
> Sermons in stones, and good in every thing.

And the sweet accents of Edgar Guest are discernible in

> If ever you have look'd on better days,
> If ever been where bells have knoll'd to church,

> If ever sat at any good man's feast,
> If ever from your eyelids wip'd a tear,
> And know what 'tis to pity, and be pitied,
> Let gentleness my strong enforcement be:

It is no wonder that Bernard Shaw has said "if nothing were left of Shakespeare but his genius, our Shakespeareolators would miss all that they admire in him." His statesmanship generally remains about the level of after-dinner political oratory:

> The heavens themselves, the planets, and this centre
> Observe degree, priority, and place,
> Insisture, course, proportion, season, form,
> Office, and custom, in all line of order:

Again—

> Therefore doth heaven divide
> The state of man in divers functions,
> Setting endeavour in continual motion;
> To which is fixed, as an aim or butt,
> Obedience: for so work the honey-bees;
> Creatures that by a rule in nature teach
> The act of order to a peopled kingdom.

So far as general ideas are concerned, Shakespeare can stand comparison with any of the choicest platitudinarians who adorn the councils of Democracy or engage the plain people of these

WILLIAM SHAKESPEARE

States through the far-scattered wisdom of syndicated editorials. There is no serious reason why people who like that sort of thing should not get it from the wood, so to speak, rather than encourage the bootlegging of the obvious—that synthetic fustian which is retailed in journalistic phials with deceptive labels. He can say these things so much better. We have heard it all before, but it sounds well when we hear:

> To-morrow, and to-morrow, and to-morrow,
> Creeps in this petty pace from day to day,
> To the last syllable of recorded time;
> And all our yesterdays have lighted fools
> The way to dusty death. Out, out, brief candle!
> Life's but a walking shadow, a poor player
> That struts and frets his hour upon the stage,
> And then is heard no more; it is a tale
> Told by an idiot, full of sound and fury,
> Signifying nothing.

As soon as the music of his craft possesses him Shakespeare forgets his rôle as the well-connected bourgeois who has seen better days; he never ceases to talk platitudes when he tries to be serious, but the words carry him away into admissions that surge up out of the depths of his being. One yawns listening to the attempted profundity of Hamlet's "To be or not to be," for "poor Will," if he had small Latin and less Greek, had not much more philosophy. Seriously serious people, like Emerson, have not been deceived by his ability to give his public "what you will." Emerson regretted "that the best poet led an obscure and profane life, using his genius for the public amusement." But out of that profanity and obscurity of his life comes all that enchants the ear in his writings. What is the pseudo-philosophy of Hamlet's soliloquy on death beside Claudio's terrorized cry in "Measure for Measure"?

> Ay, but to die, and go we know not where;
> To lie in cold obstruction and to rot;
> This sensible warm motion to become
> A kneaded clod; and the delighted spirit
> To bathe in fiery floods, or to reside
> In thrilling region of thick-ribbed ice;
> To be imprison'd in the viewless winds,
> And blown with restless violence round about
> The pendant world; or to be worse than worst
> Of those that lawless and incertain thoughts
> Imagine howling: 'tis too horrible!
> The weariest and most loathed worldly life,
> That age, ache, penury and imprisonment
> Can lay on nature, is a paradise
> To what we fear of death.

As a very solemn and very Early Victorian art critic, Mr. Ruskin, pointed out, in none of Shakespeare's thirty-seven five-act plays in blank verse is there a single hero—which is probably the best

WILLIAM SHAKESPEARE

commentary upon life that can be drawn from his writings. He has been congratulated by the professors upon his knowledge that we have each of us our station in life and should stay there; that the bee is a model for all right-thinking citizens; that Calvin Coolidge is the ideal man:

> . . . spare in diet,
> Free from gross passion or of mirth or anger,
> Constant in spirit, not swerving with the blood. . . .

that "our remedies oft in ourselves do lie"; that the qualities we should look for in our rulers are such

> As justice, verity, temperance, stableness,
> Bounty, perseverance, mercy, lowliness,
> Devotion, patience, courage, fortitude.

Very naturally the writer who could turn out this sort of thing by the yard, and do it much better than his contemporaries, "the Elizabethan blank-verse beasts" to whom Charles Lamb was addicted (in the words of Bernard Shaw) as he was addicted to gin—the writer who could do this would flourish in the theater. Anatole France has pointed out that verses spoken in the theater are always padded out with redundant and meaningless lines which are put in to fill up the intervals while the audience is digesting the words which are significant. Too much sense would overstrain the minds of the play-goers. Hence the enduring success of those Shakespearian plays—"Richard the Third," "Othello," "The Merchant of Venice," "Hamlet," "As You Like It," and "Much Ado about Nothing"—all of which lend themselves to exploitation by actor-managers and are cheerfully butchered to make a theatrical holiday from the usual trivialities. Works like "Troilus and Cressida," "All's Well that Ends Well," and "Measure for Measure," are rarely seen, as the records in England show, although doubtful rubbish like "Pericles" is included in the repertory of two of the chief exponents of Shakespeare in the modern British stage.

Thus dramatic criticism prior to the rise of the Modern Drama with Ibsen, Shaw, and the rest was not a criticism of plays (as it has since become) but of acting. Between these two stools of criticism Shakespeare has fallen to the ground, where the pedants have him at their mercy. Meanwhile his merit is diminished by the revival of the cult of the Elizabethans, whose violent, sanguinary, and obscene ranting enjoys a reflected glory from Shakespeare's preëminence. He should be read, therefore, if only as an antidote to the æsthetic posturings of the devotees of Marlowe, Webster, Tourneur, or even the occasionally poetic but never dramatic Jonson, Marston, Middleton, and Chapman. "Titus Andronicus" is a specimen of

WILLIAM SHAKESPEARE

Shakespeare's contribution to "The Tragedy of Blood"; it is one of his worst plays, but it is a masterpiece beside Webster's Bedlamite "Duchess of Malfy," Marston's delirious "Antonio's Revenge," or Cyril Tourneur's "The Revenger's Tragedy" (compared by Swinburne to Æschylus) with its eighteen violent deaths and its slaughterhouse atmosphere of lust and crime.

Shakespeare must not be read because he is the brightest star in the Elizabethan pleiad, as the enthusiasts insinuate, from Charles Lamb and Swinburne to their echoes Mr. T. S. Eliot and Rupert Brooke, but in spite of that. That "golden age" of the British theater was actually a period when the foul, the extravagant, and the horrible flourished—thanks to the hocus-pocus of blank verse, in which the record of bombastic futility was achieved. It was a period when the British theater was in a state of barbarousness compared with which the theater of France and Spain stood in the same relation as the American bathroom to a Tudor cesspool. It was, however, into this uncouth society of ranters and brawlers that Shakespeare came to learn his trade as playwright and from which he was gradually to emancipate himself—though never entirely.

The modern man can, therefore, enjoy him on condition that he be regarded as a natural genius

LITERARY BLASPHEMIES

handicapped by the conventions and conditions of an age when brawn was more respected than brains. Shakespeare does not open up the glorious world of Elizabethan literature but rather closes it by showing us the best that the times could produce. He has no message for mankind and his humor is frequently so feeble that a bad burlesque show is brilliant in comparison. Where he is unintelligible it is rarely worth while to decipher him, for the actual defects in the text have long since been repaired and the rest is merely the arid diversion of professors. If he is irresistible it is because he is a musician of words so lovely that the English tongue is forever illuminated by his use of it. Into the mouth of a savage he can put such lines as

> Be not afeared; the isle is full of noises,
> Sounds, and sweet airs, that give delight and hurt not.
> Sometimes a thousand twangling instruments
> Will hum about mine ears; and sometimes voices,
> That, if I then had wak'd after long sleep,
> Will make me sleep again: and then, in dreaming,
> The clouds methought would open and show riches
> Ready to drop upon me; that, when I wak'd
> I cried to dream again.

At the same time his attitude is essentially that of the man or woman of this skeptical age of transition, so terrifying to timorous minds. Shakespeare is hedonistic and happy in disillusion; he is Ham-

WILLIAM SHAKESPEARE

let and Falstaff, both figures that admirably represent the point of view of the civilized minority today. In the most wonderful love poetry in the world he has expressed just that combination of sensuality, passion, and cynicism which peculiarly irritates the stern mentors of our latter-day morals. He can write to his mistress:

> My mistress' eyes are nothing like the sun;
> Coral is far more red than her lips' red;
> If snow be white, why then her breasts are dun;
> If hairs be wires, black wires grow on her head.
> I have seen roses damask'd, red and white,
> But no such roses see I in her cheeks;
> And in some perfumes is there more delight
> Than in the breath that from my mistress reeks.
> I love to hear her speak; yet well I know
> That music hath a far more pleasing sound:
> I grant I never saw a goddess go—,
> My mistress, when she walks, treads on the ground;
> And yet, by heaven, I think my love as rare
> As any she belied with false compare.

The tone of disillusioned intensity is exactly in the key of the verses written to-day by a generation from which the standard-bearers of tradition retreat in order to annotate another edition of the classics—Shakespeare for preference. His own defiance of such tests as are applied—if not to him, to all in him that lives again in contemporary literature—is expressed in such phrases as

LITERARY BLASPHEMIES

> No, I am that I am, and they that level
>   At my abuses reckon up their own:
> I may be straight though they themselves be bevel;
>   By their rank thoughts my deeds must not be shown;

Orthodox Shakespeareology demands a note of deferential, reverent agnosticism in the appreciation of "poor Will." By strenuously ignoring the facts one has all the more indignation left for the faults of contemporaries. "Others abide our question—thou art free," was Matthew Arnold's apostrophe; and while these Colossi bestride the narrow world of traditional pedantic criticism, we petty men who do not take our Shakespeare sadly peep about to find reasons for that conviction which we share with him:

> Not marble, nor the gilded monuments
> Of princes, shall outlive this powerful rhyme.

Because he was of men all-too-human and of English poets the greatest, he has his place in "the wide world dreaming of things to come."

Chapter Three

JOHN MILTON

MILTON shares with Shakespeare the distinction of being the most profoundly cherished glory of English literature. In a sense his fame is even more inhumanly secure, his reputation more sacrosanct, because he liked biblical subjects in his moments of relaxation from the writing of those dreary political pamphlets which actually occupied the best years of his life and are as extinct as the conditions out of which they arose. This predilection of his for themes inspired by the Holy Scriptures has had many perhaps unpremeditated advantages for the author of "Paradise Lost," "Paradise Regained," and "Samson Agonistes." On the face of it he enjoys the inestimable advantage of being irresistibly and inevitably involved in that general confusion of unfamiliar reverence which embraces Shakespeare, the Bible and Milton in one vast inability to distinguish the source of such hallowed phrases as we owe to one or another of these treasured English classics. Such lines as "To-morrow to fresh fields and pastures new," or "Warble his native wood-notes wild," or "Casting a dim religious light," or "That last infirmity of noble minds," or "They also serve who only stand and wait," or "Better to reign in hell than serve in heaven," have the charm of that familiarity which breeds indifference to their authorship.

The second advantage attributable to Milton's scriptural themes is the ease with which they dispense with the necessity for reading him. The sacred nature of the subject insures respect, while the fortunate compulsion to attend Sunday school which parents even to-day exercise upon their children equally insures a knowledge of the rudiments, at least, of the subject itself. For a writer so thoroughly unread as Milton, in whom neither actor managers nor movie magnates can seek consolation, the benefits of biblical association cannot be overstressed. Even Dante with his "Inferno" presupposes a slightly higher degree of theological education than is demanded for the instantaneous recognition of the theme of "Paradise Lost." As a matter of fact, the professors and annotators themselves have tacitly recognized the fact that Milton is one of those great authors who should be seen but not heard. Statisticians love to dwell upon the vast literature which has accumulated about Shakespeare. By comparison, Milton dwells in splendid isolation from exegetists. There is only one standard work on Milton, but it does consist, I admit, of six octavo volumes, making a total of some five thousand pages. This monumental achievement, which brightened the life of Professor Masson from 1859 to 1880, has daunted even his colleagues ever since. Milton has not proved such a happy hunting-ground for pundits as Shakespeare.

The suspicious, therefore, are entitled to wonder if a great author whom only one professor has resolutely tackled is not beyond the finite literary capacity of the plain people. Granting that one must go through the motions of having some acquaintance with the Bard, if only to qualify for admission to Shakespearian revivals, there does not seem to be any corresponding compulsion to deprive the happy few of their exclusive delight in the works of John Milton. Even those six octavo volumes are difficult to procure and most expensive, whereas *Shakespeare: His Mind and Art* and Sir Sidney Lee's *Life of Shakespeare* are in every schoolboy's satchel. Can it be that Samuel Johnson was right when he declared, with his usual hearty English frankness, that " 'Paradise Lost' is one of the books which the reader admires and lays down, and forgets to take up again. No one ever wished it longer than it is. Its perusal is a duty rather than a pleasure"?

It must be said at the outset that Milton did not make a very happy entrance into the world of English poetry. When he was fifteen he wrote a version of the One Hundred and Thirty-Sixth Psalm, which begins

> Let us, with gladsome mind
> Praise the Lord, for he is kind:
> For his mercies aye endure,
> Ever faithful, ever sure.

Here we have a piece of hymn-book verse typical of hundreds which have driven English hymnologists of taste to cry out in despair. Not more reassuring is the fact that his first original English poem is addressed to "A Fair Infant Dying of a cough," from which it seems that the pulmonary trouble of the deceased was due to the fact that Bleak Winter

> . . . being amorous on that lovely dye
> That did thy cheek envermeil, thought to kiss
> But killed, alas! and then bewailed his fatal bliss.

In the circumstances it is not surprising that he declared, on leaving college, with both truth and poetry,

JOHN MILTON

> How soon hath Time, the subtle thief of youth,
> Stol'n on his wing my three-and-twentieth year!
> My hasting days fly on with full career,
> But my late spring no hid or blossom shew'th.

After which he retired to the country to prepare himself for "Paradise Lost," for, in spite of his "late spring," Milton conceived himself as having the vocation of a poet and he set about becoming a poet with the gravity of a pedant qualifying for a learned profession. Very naturally he wrote about a child dying of a cough at an age when Shakespeare had written "Venus and Adonis." The latter went off to London at twenty-two unconscious of "amplitude of mind to greatest deeds," and merely produced such youthful follies as "Romeo and Juliet," "A Midsummer-Night's Dream" and his "Rape of Lucrece." Milton's procedure was, of course, different. After seven years at Christ's College, Cambridge, during which he had written about the baby's cough, he withdrew for five years to his father's house in a village a few miles from London. To quote his own words

> And wisdom's self
> Oft seeks to sweet retired solitude,
> Where with her best nurse, contemplation,
> She plumes her feathers and lets grow her wings
> That in the various bustle of resort
> Were all-too ruffled and sometimes impair'd.

LITERARY BLASPHEMIES

To this p e r i o d of preparation belong "L'Allegro," "Il Penseroso," "Comus," and "Lycidas," which the "Lady of Christ's," as they called him at Cambridge, produced from his unruffled and prolonged meditations and studies. Notwithstanding the latter, he entitles one of these works, "Il Penseroso," a non-existent Italian word, whose correct form, "pensieroso," does not mean what Milton meant. Notwithstanding the country life, far from the "bustle of resort," the images and references to nature in his poetry nature are "impair'd" to the extent of showing us a skylark coming to the poet's window, an eglantine that is "twisted," a "wan" cowslip, a pine "rooted deep," and primroses, woodbine, daffodils, and jasmine all in flower simultaneously. Even the lightning is made to "singe" the tree tops and the elm is described as a tree with foliage so thick as to be "starproof." It is fortunate that Shakespeare devoted the same years of his life in London to the coarse business of living, so that his geography and his history, his Latin and his Greek, suffered, but he had the spontaneity of the true poet, instead of the bookish ecstasies of a serious young man with a poetic vocation, a call, so to speak, to the ministry of the Muses.

The harvest of Milton's early poems is meager, but there we must seek, nevertheless, whatever is of compelling interest in him. The great work of his life was at this stage far off, and so much intervened that, by the time he came to write "Paradise Lost" and "Paradise Regained," he was a disgruntled Puritan trying to remember that he once was a poet. Whereas now he is a potential poet who occasionally forgets to be a Puritan. Sometimes he could say

> Alas! What boots it with uncessant care
> To tend the homely slighted Sheperd's trade,
> And strictly meditate the thankless Muse,
> Were it not better do as others use,
> To sport with Amaryllis in the shade,
> Or with the tangles of Neæra's hair?

And we find him crying

> Haste thee, nymph, and bring with thee
> Jest and youthful jollity,
> Quips and Cranks and wanton Wiles,
> Nods, and Becks, and wreathed Smiles,
> Such as hang on Hebe's cheek,
> And love to live in dimple sleek;
> Sport that wrinkled Care derides
> And Laughter holding both his sides.
> Come, and trip it as ye go
> On the light fantastic toe.

He could remember "spicy, nut-brown ale," "Ladies, whose bright eyes rain influence," and even that abhorrent resort, the theater:

> Then to the well-trod stage anon,
> If Jonson's learned sock be on,
> Or sweetest Shakespeare, fancy's child,
> Warble his native wood-notes wild.

At such moments he realized the impulse to poetry:

> Lap me in soft Lydian airs
> Married to immortal verse
> Such as the meeting soul may pierce
> In notes with many a winding bout
> Of linked sweetness long drawn out.

The few lines and phrases which enjoy the genuine immortality of incorporation into current cultivated usage come, with few exceptions from "Comus," "Lycidas," "L'Allegro," and "Il Penseroso." As I have said, even then, they are usually attributed to the Bible or Shakespeare. The professors, of course, insist that these works are merely preparatory to those that one praises but never reads.

In this view, to do them justice, Milton would have probably agreed, for he took his poetry sadly, as the English are said to take their pleasures, and found his greatest inspiration in "divinest Melancholy," "Goddess sage and holy." After writing these poems of his first period, he made a tour in Italy, and during the year or so of his absence, as

JOHN MILTON

he proudly declared, his conduct was as irreproachable as if he had stayed at home, a precedent hardly followed in modern times by upholders of the harsher traditions of Anglo-Saxon pudicity. He did, however, soften under the charm of the South, as so many great English poets did after him. In Italian, which, as Mr. Anthony Comstock pointed out, is the language of lust, he wrote five poems about a dark-haired beauty whose "majestic movements and love-darting dark brow" impressed him, accustomed as he was to blondes with "golden nets of hair" and "vermeil-tinctur'd cheek." Having called upon Galileo, who was living under the surveillance of the Holy Inquisition, and, generally speaking, having satisfied himself that it was a grand and glorious feeling to be an English Protestant, Milton returned to England, where the Civil War was brewing.

The war broke out in 1642, three years after his homecoming, and it had been under way less than twelve months when Milton departed from London for a month, returning with a wife, the daughter of a Cavalier. The girl was not an intellectual and she was not a Puritan; the result was inevitable—she left him. The "bashful muteness of a virgin" turned out to be "unliveliness and natural sloth unfit for conversation," a remarkable commentary from a man who had published his views upon the reform of education, excluding women from its benefits, and whose ideal, "He for God only, she for God in him," could hardly prove very alluring to a girl of seventeen brought away from a gay Cavalier household to the austere home of a Puritan. Milton at once proceeded with the publication of one of the famous and mostly forgotten tracts which occupied the twenty years of his prime, from 1641 to 1660—the period of the rise, apotheosis, and downfall of the Puritan revolution. The pamphlet on *The Doctrine and Discipline of Divorce* actually seems to have been begun by him on his honeymoon, and is typical of his activities as a pamphleteer. It was prompted entirely by his personal grievances and it was utterly ineffectual. The English Parliament had other matters to attend to before taking up Milton's demand for a divorce from Mary Powell. It is true, a lady preacher whose husband "was unsanctified" and did not "speak the language of Canaan," and who was away with the army, read Milton to such good purpose that she contracted an impromptu marriage with her fellow-pastor, William Jenney, to the great scandal of the Presbyterians. Three more divorce pamphlets failed to move the Parliament, although Milton threatened the law with "the censure of the consequences," if it failed to assist him in his courtship of "a very handsome and

JOHN MILTON

witty Miss Davis," to whom he was paying his addresses while Mary stayed away with her parents. The problem solved itself by the reversal of the Royalist fortunes and the reconciliation of the Powell family with their Puritan and therefore helpful son-in-law.

Even in the classroom I doubt if Milton's divorce tracts are supposed to be part of a gentleman's library, but his pamphlet on the liberty of the press receives even to-day the homage which vice pays to virtue. *Areopagitica: a Speech for the Liberty of Unlicensed Printing* is not, it so happens, an argument in favor of freedom of speech. Like the divorce pamphlets, it is concerned with a specific grievance of the author himself, and was written, not on behalf of any principle, but in defence of his own failure to procure a license from the reverend gentlemen whose duty it was to see that no "forged, scandalous, seditious, libellous and unlicensed" publications were issued. They would naturally not license his divorce pamphlets, so, with that charming respect for law and order peculiar to ascetic and disciplinarian reformers, Milton had defied the law. The title of this pamphlet is borrowed from Socrates, with whose *Areopagitic Discourse* it has nothing in common as regards form or content. I suspect its survival is due to the fact that it is the one document that it is possible to read out of the mass of cheap political hack writing and topical propaganda upon which Milton lavished the years for which, as we have seen, he had so carefully prepared himself to live the life of a great poet. It must also be said that it contains that kind of pithy platitude so sound as to be meaningless, which has always been the mainstay of Anglo-Saxon rhetoric. Let us note a few: "A dram of well-doing should be preferred before many times as much the forcible hindrance of evil doing." "Opinion in good men is but knowledge in the making." "As good almost kill a man as kill a good book." Such apophthegms have the wearing quality and durability which enable judges to quote the first while jailing radicals; clergymen to quote the second while conscientious objectors are being lynched; and the third to evoke thunder of applause at some meeting of authors who have refused to move a finger in defence of a work being harried by professional moralists.

Meanwhile the Civil War was progressing towards the execution of Charles I and the triumph of Presbyterianism. Milton remarked that "New Presbyter is but old Priest writ large," but beyond this he had nothing to say of the slightest importance either to those interested in literature or ideas. He had a great opportunity to come forward in defence of real freedom of thought, but

JOHN MILTON

the Presbyterians "did not fine or imprison him, or put him out of the synagogue," as one of his biographers ingenuously remarks, so very naturally John Milton did not receive any call from on high to strike a blow for liberty—his own interests were not seriously affected. After the king was beheaded, however, he wrote his famous exposition of the complete gospel of Ku-Kluxism, *The Tenure of Kings and Magistrates,* in which he lays down the principle of lynch law that "any who has the power" may interfere to discharge duties which the lawful authorities are supposed to have neglected. He wrote other scurrilous pamphlets after his appointment as Latin secretary, upon which the handbooks of literature lavish whatever praise professorial fancy dictates. "Humane studies were swamped in a biblical brawl," to quote one of Milton's biographers, who differs from his academic colleagues in admitting the waste and the irony of this phase of the author's activities. Milton actually lost his eyesight rather than abandon these written squabbles in Latin and English, in which he reveals himself as only a more proficient classical scholar than the most boorish zealot in Cromwell's army who ever speared a Papist in Ireland. At the age of forty-three he went blind, and he had not even begun his masterpiece. He had, however, written *Eikonoklastes,* in which he sneers at

Charles I for having read Shakespeare, and dismisses Sidney's "Arcadia" as "a vain amatorious poem."

Apart from his political writings, no verse of any note came from him during the period of the Puritan revolution, unless one count the doggerel into which he turned the Psalms. In order to please the Puritans, who, with their accustomed fine taste in such matters, preferred ballad rhymes to the antistrophic lyrics as rendered in the Book of Common Prayer, Milton put no less than seventeen Psalms into verse. He had not even the excuse of compulsion, and there were numerous rivals for the honor of mutilating fine literature. His first and second wives had died, and his daughters had not yet grown up to hate him, but his youngest nephew, whom he had educated, was the author of a work which the authorities found to contain "much lascivious and profane matter." Another nephew had written a book calculated, it seems, "to debauch the manners of the nation, and to bring back the King." It was evident that Milton's system of education had not worked, or rather had worked as repression always does. His nephews frequented "Cavaliers, and *bon vivans* and demireps." Neither for the Puritan nor for the poet were circumstances very propitious in 1660, when the monarchy was restored, just as Milton was writing

JOHN MILTON

his final tract showing a *Ready and Easy Way to Establish a Free Commonwealth*.

In his fifty-second year, therefore, blind, poor, his occupation gone, Milton settled down to write the great works upon which his fame rests. He married a third time, shortly after the Restoration, and as his daughters grew older they were taught to read aloud in six languages and to help their father, who refused, however, to allow them to learn the languages so that they might understand them. These ladies detested him cordially, and one of them remarked that his death would have been news, but that his marriage hardly merited the term. A system of education and a revolt quite in keeping with Milton's view that

> Nothing lovelier can be found
> In woman, than to study household good,

but a somewhat ironical footnote on the lines much admired in academic circles as a lofty tribute to women:

> All higher knowledge in her presence falls
> Degraded; wisdom in discourse with her
> Loses discountenanc'd, and like folly shows;
> Authority and reason on her wait,
> As one intended first, not after made.

It was Milton's first intention to take some theme

of Arthurian romance as the subject of his epic, but he discarded this idea when he realized that the stories of King Arthur and the Round Table were not all gospel truth. He required a subject whose authenticity was established beyond doubt, and so, being a Calvinist, he had recourse, not to the Gospels, but to the Old Testament, where he fancied poetry and Fundamentalism could be happily combined. But, as I have said, he waited so long before putting his plan into execution that the Elizabethan elements which lent a reflected glory to his early work had long since vanished before the harsh fervors of militant Puritanism. "Paradise Lost" and "Paradise Regained" contained more Fundamentalism than poetry. Milton could compromise upon such trifling details as the Ptolemaic and Copernican systems of astronomy, so that his universe is simultaneously heliocentric and geocentric, in spite of his meeting with Galileo, but he could not evade the injunctions of Calvinistic theology. Never was an epic conceived with more grotesque and depressing intent than "to justify the ways of God to men." That is not the stuff of which the dreams of the world's great epics have been made.

Milton objected to poetry which came "from the heat of youth, or the vapors of wine, like that which flows at waste from the pen of some vulgar encomiast, or the trencher fury of a rhyming parasite"—a dictum which eliminates almost all the great poets of the world, from Homer to Verlaine. His own view of the poetic mission was "to inbreed and cherish in a great people the seeds of virtue . . . to set the affections in right tune . . . to sing victorious agonies of martyrs and saints, the deeds and triumphs of just and pious nations . . . to deplore the general relapses of Kingdoms and States from justice and God's true worship"—a definition which points towards the perfection and popularity of Robert W. Service and Ella Wheeler Wilcox, to mention the two great song birds of evangelical democracy to-day. Holding such opinions and being the man of his age that he was, Milton inevitably, "after long choosing and beginning late," selected the Fall of Man for his subject, and undertook to explain and solve the mystery of human existence. The result is the vast, chaotic, allegorical, biblical, mythological, bookish, and topical narrative poem of seventeenth century Puritanism, "Paradise Lost," in which, as Ruskin said, "every artifice of convention is consciously employed—not a single fact being conceived as tenable by any living faith."

A fact overlooked by all the commentators, until Dr. George Sigerson pointed it out in 1922, is that Milton seems to have been facilitated in his choice of a subject by the *Carmen Paschale* of Sedulius, which was first published in 1475 and went through many editions. From the parallels established by this scholar between Sedulius and Milton it is evident that the latter had no right to claim to have pursued "things unattempted yet in prose or rhyme"—the phrase itself being a translation of Ariosto's *"Cosa non detta in prosa mai nè in rima."* For example, Milton:

> Of man's first disobedience and the fruit
> Of that forbidden tree whose mortal taste
> Brought death into the world, and all our woe,
> With loss of Eden,

which is a paraphrase of Sedulius:

> The first of man, by ruthless serpent cast
> From Eden's flowerful seat, woeful, at last
> In lures of pleasant taste drank bitter death.
> Nor he alone, presumptuous cause of wrath,
> Fell 'neath the mortal law, but all of man
> The sequent race who all in him began.

Dr. Sigerson traces the epics of Milton and Sedulius step by step, from the start to the finish, pointing out parallels for every turn of the narrative. It is not a question of mere isolated coincidences of thought and language. The whole structure, thought structure and word structure, in Milton is imitative. "Paradise Regained" is differentiated from its sketch model in Sedulius only by the long-winded speeches of the devil. The relative failure of this poem is explained by the fact that "Milton had found but one precedent and consequently had to fill out the simple and sufficient structure of Sedulius with interminable speeches" —more than half of the first three books, to be exact. When there are other precedents, as in the case of "Paradise Lost" the decorations are supplied not only by borrowings from the Latin and Greek classics, but also from three other sources.

The scenes concerned with the creation and the early history of man were taken by Milton from three Christian Latin poets, Dracontius, Victor and Avitus, who flourished at the close of the fifth century. From the first of these, as Dr. Sigerson shows by copious quotation, comes the celebrated apostrophe to light in "Paradise Lost." From Victor Milton took his description of Paradise, its loss, the banishment of Adam and Eve, their despair and their repentance. Finally in Avitus he found the idyll of the first nuptials, and the figure of Satan, gazing on their innocent existence, filled with rage, envy and humiliation, and resolving to wreck the handiwork of God.

The theme was chosen, as all the learned commentators prefer to explain, because it was truth, not fiction. It was addressed to an audience who shared the author's beliefs, and who respected the work because they thought it was a profound and beautiful interpretation of life. To a modern audience no such appeal can be made; we are asked to acquiesce not in beliefs but in illusions, whose absurdity, even within their own limits, is accentuated by the author's total lack of humor, his unnecessary ignorance, and his incongruous pedantry. Even Milton's academic admirers have not dared to deny the innumerable and radical defects in "Paradise Lost" and "Paradise Regained." Although they insist upon the reality of the subject as justifying its choice, they entreat us to remember that we are in a mythological world. They declare that the mythology and demonology of Milton are obsolete, but ask us to surrender to an interest which they inspired only when they were real, vital matters of faith. On the principle of grasping a nettle they concede all the objections which might be raised by an intelligent reader, and then take refuge in the sublimity of the style and the pathetic circumstances of the blind author in his loneliness and neglect, with the ribald laughter of the bright Restoration period mocking the dreary experiment of making men moral by terrorism.

The nettle of classical English literature needs to be firmly grasped by the professors, for succeed-

JOHN MILTON

ing generations have been more and more repelled by its prickly Puritanism and its blistering pedantry. Adam and Eve are a typical Puritan ménage of the period, of whom a French critic has said: "Good heavens! make them put on their clothes at once! Such nice people would immediately have invented trousers and prudery." When Eve succumbs to temptation her sentiments do her credit:

> And from that time see
> How beauty is excell'd by manly grace,
> And wisdom which alone is truly fair.

Adam is a model of all that a virtuous Puritan householder should be

> Fair consort, the hour
> Of night and all things now retired to rest
> Mind us of like repose; since God hath set
> Labour and rest, as day and night, to men
> Successive; and the timely dew of sleep,
> Now falling with soft slumbrous weight, inclines
> Our eyelids. Other creatures all day long
> Rove idle, unemployed, and less need rest.

He even indulges his spouse in a brief dissertation upon the interpretation of dreams, which proves, according to all the rules of pedantic annotation, that Milton anticipated Freud when he wrote:

LITERARY BLASPHEMIES

> Know that in the soul
> Are many lesser faculties that serve
> Reason as chief; among these Fancy next
> Her office holds; of all external things,
> Which the five watchful senses represent,
> She forms imaginations, aery shapes,
> Which Reason joining or disjoining, frames
> All what we affirm or deny, and call
> Our knowledge and opinion. . . .
> Oft in her absence, mimic Fancy wakes
> To imitate her; but, misjoining shapes,
> Wild work produces oft, and most in dreams. . . .

The same commentator, if American, might also see some prophetic connotations in the line, which occurs when the Serpent seduces Eve by his syllogisms,

> Such prohibitions bind not.

With Calvanistic forethought God sends Raphael to warn Adam that he is about to sin

> Lest, wilfully transgressing, he pretend
> Surprisal, unadmonish'd, unforewarn'd.

If Adam and Eve are a respectable, bourgeois, Puritan couple, Heaven is, as one critic calls it, "a celestial barracks" in which God resembles a well-behaved Stuart King. Discourses, arguments and homilies in the approved, arid manner of the

JOHN MILTON

time replace the wonder and mystery with which great poets have invested their visions of the supernatural. The Angels have good appetites, and cold meats are eaten so that the food may not spoil while the syllogists harangue each other. Eve is shown to be a dutiful wife who prefers her husband's opinions to those of any stranger. Milton's memory for parallels from classical literature reminds one of school days when any given English sentence for Latin composition at once aroused the corresponding wooden and eternal idiomatic form in Bradley's "Latin Grammar," which was duly employed whatever the English variant might be. Satan's shield is compared to the moon because Homer so compared the shield of Achilles, and in imitation of Homer again he sets out the names of the angels' leaders, with full particulars as to their territories, and it turns out that they are precisely the heathen gods of another age. It is not surprising that the translator of Omar Khayyam, more widely read in English to-day than anything of Milton's, declared that the pedantry of "Paradise Lost" "tipped me at once out of paradise or even hell into the schoolroom, worse than either."

Adam is obviously too respectable an English bourgeois to be the hero of an epic, and thus we come to the supreme irony of "Paradise Lost," to wit, that Lucifer is the finest character in it.

LITERARY BLASPHEMIES

The first four books of the poem, in which the story of Satan is narrated as consecutively as is possible for Milton, are those which the conventional usually have in mind when they profess their undying admiration for Milton. The remaining eight are generally forgotten and, if the truth must be known, only the first two books of the four in question have that claim to be remembered which consists in the fact that they can be read without excessive effort. Theology is reduced to a minimum and four more or less engaging scoundrels, Lucifer, Belial, Moloch, and Mammon, impress the impartial reader as personages of brilliant intellect, quite human vindictiveness, or urbane common sense. Hitherto in English literature the devil had been the conventional medieval clown, with horns and cloven feet, but Milton introduces us to a gentleman, or rather a superman, who is none the worse for being modeled very probably upon the defeated Cromwell, who, at least to Milton, seemed to incarnate the virtues of a strong man in defeat:

> The unconquerable will
> And study of revenge, immortal hate,
> And courage never to submit or yield,
> And what is else not to be overcome:
> That glory never shall his wrath or might
> Extort from me.

JOHN MILTON

It is Satan who displays courage, resource, and inventiveness, who uses that artillery in heaven to which the pundits take exception, having swallowed so many camels that this gnat disturbs them; who heads the revolt of man against God, and wins to his side a third of the angels and almost all the sons of Adam. It is the Devil, too, who voices the principles of the Puritans, who fled to New England and were, in Milton's day, confronted by a wild and savage territory to be tamed and cultivated.

> Is this the region, this the soil, the clime,
> Said then the lost Archangel, this the seat
> That we must change for Heav'n? this mournful gloom
> For that celestial light
> . . . .
>   Here, at least,
> We shall be free; th' Almighty, hath not built
> Here for his envy; will not drive us hence:
> Here we may reign secure;

Just as Cromwell supplied to Puritan hero-worship the hint from which Lucifer evolved, so the plight of the angels cast out from Paradise was suggested by the great adventure of the Puritans who landed at Plymouth Rock. As a distinguished exponent of New England tradition repeatedly points out, "it was no such abstract love of ideal liberty as the superstitious traditions of our later democracy have fondly ascribed to them, which led them painfully to seek refuge in what Cotton Mather fitly called the solitudes of an American desert. . . . There was never a temper much less tolerant than that which they implanted at first in their continent of forest and wilderness. They cared as little for abstract liberty as Strafford cared, or Laud, or Charles himself." Professor Barrett Wendell, whose words I have quoted, was a fervent admirer of Milton, but his conclusion was that "the great and lasting human expression of Elizabethan Puritanism" is not to be found in literature, but "in the planting of New England, and in the still vital historical growth which has sprung from that seed."

Here we come upon a clue to the mystery of Milton's fame, and to the curious pertinacity with which the mandarins of literary tradition simultaneously give him away, yet insist that he must be taken whole and admired without stint or limit. They make no such appeals *ad misericordiam* for Shakespeare, or, indeed, any other great classic. As I have already shown, so far from conceding that Shakespeare had faults, they have made a plaster saint out of him and have taken all precautions to render him as dull as he seems to them. Perhaps it is in order to show that they *have* read Milton, whereas the plain people universally take him for granted, that they dive into his vast work, "outrageous as a sea, dark, wasteful, wild," and come up to the surface bearing evidence of his weaknesses and incongruities.

My own view is that Milton's fame rests upon the simple fact that, instead of joining the witch-hunters in Salem, he stayed at home and became the one great poet Puritanism has produced. As such he has the rarity and interest of those strange antediluvian reconstructions which adorn the prehistoric departments of museums for the amazement of gaping crowds on Sunday afternoons. Just as they are not in a position to criticize what purports to be an ichthyosaurus, so they accept on trust the assurances of Milton's grandeur. Grandeur and sublimity are words with which to conjure in all discussions of Milton, but they are merely elements of great poetry; they are not sufficient. The Reverend Mark Pattison, B.D., a divine and an Oxford Don, who cannot certainly be accused of bias against the subject of "Paradise Lost," says, nevertheless, that the "failure of vital power in the constitution of the poem is due to the very selection of the subject; had he remembered the principle of the Aristotelean Poetic (which he otherwise highly prized), that men in action are the poet's proper theme, he would have raised his imaginative fabric on a more permanent foundation; upon the appetites, passions, and emotions of men, their vices and virtues, their aims and ambitions, which are a far more constant quantity than any theological system."

In other words, if Milton had been more truly an Elizabethan and less incurably a Puritan, his work would be immortal, as much more antiquated and primitive poetry is, and he would have been a great poet. Homer and Vergil incorporated into their epics beliefs and customs at which we have smiled for centuries, but they sang of eternal things, of love and war and death; they were not in possession of revealed truth, and are thus without the personal limitations destroying vision and thwarting impulse, which hemmed in the faint early trickle of genuine poetry in Milton, as they have increasingly repulsed readers from his obsolete and artificial works. He has been compared to a river flowing between two different territories and colored by their different earth. At the end of the Elizabethan age he caught its last breath of poetry, and this he deferred using until it was little more than an intermittent respiration, heard in such lines —even in "Paradise Lost"—as

> Now comes still evening on, and twilight grey
> Had in her sober livery all things clad;
> Silence accompanied; for beast and bird,
> They to their grassy couch, these to their nests,

JOHN MILTON

Were slunk, all but the wakeful nightingale;
She all night long her amorous descant sung;
Silence was pleased: now glowed the firmament
With living sapphires; Hesperus that led
The starry host rose brightest, till the moon
Rising in clouded majesty, at length
Apparent queen unveiled her peerless light
And o'er the dark her silver mantle drew.

He belonged to a drab age and elected to write the only kind of epic of which such an age is capable; he was a Puritan zealot, whose services as a political pamphleteer produced only two prose works which are distinguishable from the dusty mass of such tracts as the Civil War inspired. Neither of these sprang from any understanding of liberty, but were apologies and pleas for his own conduct as a husband and an author who was defying the law, or contemplated doing so. Although his divorce tracts and the *Areopagitica* are mentioned as examples of his devotion to liberty, nobody has ever pretended that the work upon which his best energies were expended is other than that which might have come from any fanatical and scurrilous champion of the Revolution and Commonwealth. His poems are remembered, therefore, merely because of that Elizabethan element in him, belonging to a time when England surrendered to her sensibilities and to the free play of the imagination, holding to natural beliefs, full-blooded and adventurous, pagan and wild, responding instinctively to beauty, if not always capable of expressing it. As against Sidney, Shakespeare, and Spenser, Puritan England can set only Milton, and he is buttressed up by so many concessions that one detects a fearful anxiety lest his claim be completely dismissed.

Milton, then, remains as a sacred relic of the belief that Puritanism and literature can be harmoniously reconciled. He lived on into an age which reversed in life and literature everything that he and his supporters, both contemporary and posthumous, have advocated. It is significant that, while even clerical commentators admit that time is sapping such vitality as his most important works possessed, revivals of the gay comedies of the Restoration are being played to-day to crowded audiences, who heard nothing of Congreve, Farquhar, and Vanbrugh from the college exegetists, unless perhaps that they were unworthy of serious attention. Restoration drama by its innate vital qualities will survive, and the names of its creators will become as familiar through experience to modern playgoers as the names of immortally dead classics are familiar to professors. Annotators are not required to explain why "The Way of the World" is charming after centuries of neglect. They are essential to the spread of Milton's fame, for he illustrates more perfectly than any other the process of artificial respiration whereby classical literature is kept alive. By the average man or woman of the present day he is likely to be remembered because of this one characteristic, which he had in common with all Puritans: he made the Devil irresistibly attractive.

Chapter Four

JONATHAN SWIFT

AFTER the cloistered fame of Milton and the too remote and overpowering glory of Shakespeare, the luminous English eighteenth century opens for us with a work whose vitality and enduring popularity place it beyond the need of artificial academic respiration. *Gulliver's Travels* is a living classic of such universal appeal, it has been spread abroad in so many editions and translations, that it has taken on something of the anonymity of a legend or folk-tale, existing outside of critical time and space. Children all over the world have followed Captain Gulliver's adventures amongst the Lilliputians, and their elders have watched or shared their amusement without pondering too deeply on the significance of the innocent work. Thus it has been passed off as a juvenile masterpiece, and classed with the dreary *Pilgrim's Progress* and the moralizing *Robinson Crusoe* as a book for the edification of the young. In maintaining this polite fiction great assistance has been derived from the literary mandarins, who have made a bogey of Jonathan Swift and have entreated all who would listen to avert the eyes chastely from the horrors concealed beneath the deceptive surface of Swift's works.

The method by which this end has been accomplished is twofold: Swift's own life has been held up as an awful warning, and his work has been put away on the top shelves of the library, amid shuddering allusions intended to console us for the substitution of popular bowdlerizations of *Gulliver's Travels*. "No fouler pen than Swift's has soiled our literature. His language is horrible from first to last. He is full of odious images, of base and abominable allusions. It would be a labor of Hercules to cleanse his pages. His love-letters are defaced by his incurable coarseness. . . . It is a question not of morality, but of decency, whether it is becoming to sit in the same room with this divine. . . . In this matter Swift is inexcusable." Thus in characteristic terms does one of these "bloodless persons of good taste"—to borrow an appropriate French phrase—undertake to frighten away the unwary. Having done so, he then meditates upon the irony of fate which has turned into "a child's book and a suitable Christmas present" a work which was Swift's "gospel of hatred, his testament of woe, upon which he expended the treasures of his wit, and into which he instilled the concentrated essence of his rage."

The great ironist himself would have thoroughly appreciated this irony, but it may be doubted if he would have had much difficulty in explaining it. The recoil from his ideas fits in very naturally with this conception of human intelligence: "Expect no more from man than such an animal is capable of, and you will every day find my description of the Yahoos more resembling." One of the first things that Swift did not expect from such an animal was intellectual courage, and intelligence was not precisely the outstanding characteristic of "the most pernicious race of little odious vermin that Nature ever suffered to crawl upon the face of the earth." Consequently, the contortions of the commentators who have relegated *Gulliver's Travels* to the nursery are not without their humor. "It has no moral, no social, no philosophical purpose. It was the mere ebullition of cynicism and misanthropy. A savage *jeu d'esprit*. And as such wise men will regard it. Against this dictum of Professor Churton Collins there stands, of course, the awkward fact that Swift's greatest contemporaries admired and appreciated this work; that the most intelligent and civilized of all literary worlds—that of the eighteenth century—had no hesitation in enjoying "so merry a book," which

JONATHAN SWIFT

"was universally read—from the Cabinet Council to the Nursery," to quote the author of "The Beggar's Opera." Moreover, as a horrified critic of to-day reminds us, "Maids of Honour chuckled loudest over those very passages for which buyers [of modern editions] will look in vain." In the circumstances, all that the professor can say is: "At no period distinguished by generosity of sentiment, by humanity, by decency, could such a satire have been universally applauded. Yet so it was. The men and women of those times appear to have seen nothing objectionable in an apologue which would scarcely have passed without protest in the Rome of Petronius."

This disarming innocence concerning the Rome of Petronius would seem to imply that Professor Collins read his Satyricon in an edition as effectively denaturized as those currently sold of *Gulliver's Travels*. Perish the eighteenth century, provided injustice be done to Swift! As he himself said, "when a great genius appears in the world, the dunces are all in confederacy against him." He lacked that discretion which he defined as "a species of lower prudence, by the assistance of which people of the meanest intelligence, without any other qualification, pass through the world in great tranquillity and with universal good treatment, neither giving nor taking offence." His attitude towards life did not allow of his being fitted into any of the categories to which Anglo-Saxon optimism incessantly strives to reduce all the spiritual currents of English literature: constructive energy, moralistic good sense, and a genial tonic humor. Although his birth in Ireland was an accident, he was the first great Irishman in English literature, for his Anglo-Irish origins are typical of almost all the best-known Irish men of letters who have succeeded him down to our own day. It is not for nothing that we find in him so many of the qualities that have come to be particularly identified with Anglo-Irish literature, from the political challenge to England in his own writings (and in those of his contemporary, Bishop Berkeley) to the paradoxes of Oscar Wilde, the rationalistic irony of Bernard Shaw, and the harsh Rabelaisianism—without the mirth of Rabelais—of James Joyce.

In the year 1667, when Jonathan Swift was born in Dublin, Milton published "Paradise Lost"; but the Puritan epoch, as well as the last faint echoes of Elizabethan poetry, had disappeared when the eighteenth century opened, and it was most appropriately not until then that Swift's first book was published, *A Tale of a Tub,* in 1704. He thus inaugurated the Augustan age, which was the age of great English prose, during which

JONATHAN SWIFT

modern literature—as it is commonly understood to-day—was born in the novel, the essay, and the periodical. The first of the moderns, Swift belonged peculiarly to that age of reason which, in spite of all that has intervened—the rise of Romanticism, of industrialism, of democracy—is the nearest classical period to our own time, nearer than nineteenth-century Victorianism, and with an immediate appeal to us which none of the earlier periods of English literature can have for any but scholars. It was a time, like the present, of questioning and skepticism, of transition. Deism and free thought were stripping religion of its mysticism and the philosophers were seeking new principles; while moral, ethical, and political concepts were subjected to the deflating process of rational analysis illuminated by wit. Poetry contented itself with rigid classic formulæ, for prose was the instrument which was perfected to correspond to the intimate needs of a society which found its fullest expression in satire, criticism, and journalism. It was an age without faith—consumed by a desire for clarity, logic, and exact thinking; but below the surface one discerns the deep undertone which was to swell out, as the eighteenth century closed, into the American and French Revolutions and the mystical romanticism and humanitarianism of the beginning of the nineteenth century. Then came the dark night of industrial democracy, when plumbing and profits became the natural tests of progress and civilization.

All the elements of the eighteenth century seem to reach their maximum of intensity in the person of Jonathan Swift. The contrast between latent passion and inexorable reason produces in him a profound and tortured spiritual antithesis, and the drama of feeling and thought reaches heights of tragedy in his life, of which little or nothing transpires in his works. Swift never betrays himself; he never loses his hold upon his emotions. His prose is the tersest and lightest; more perhaps than Defoe and Dryden he is the father of modern English. He anticipates the great pessimists of modern literature—Leopardi, Schopenhauer, and Nietzsche—for his doubts are deeper and more radical than those of Voltaire and the French philosophers who made the French Revolution possible. While the form of his work, the ease of his wit are essentially of his own century his doubting scrutiny sees far beyond temporary, local, and surface foibles; and while he portrays these he also tears aside all the veils of sentiment and fiction which disguise mankind and conceal us from ourselves. When he reduced the human race to the level of Yahoos he gave us a word with which we still describe the elemental creature which slumbers in all of us and emerges on such little provocation that we usually disguise its collective manifestations, at least, with some lofty ideal. As in literature, so in life we cannot stand a truth which "banishes from decent households a fourth part of one of the most brilliant and delightful of English books," to quote Sir Edmund Gosse's criticism of the last part of *Gulliver's Travels*.

As the supreme expression of an age which was a defiance of all the ideals and conventions of the modern industrial era, but which curiously corresponds to this present time of transition when the moralities, no less than the practical achievements of that era, have been definitely shaken out of their complacency—Swift is a problem for the champions of utilitarian Christianity. The bulk of his writings are inaccessible, and on the literary map their whereabouts is indicated by the ancient superscription of fear and ignorance: "Here are lions." We may have him as the author of a child's book, or not at all, and in order to dampen whatever enthusiasm or curiosity might prompt the average reader to go further, Swift's personal career has been exhibited with much rumbling of stage thunder and melodramatic indignation and wiping away of crocodile tears. Apart from the literary handbooks—which provide what might be termed the broadcasting of the actual performances—we have the performers themselves, including some of the most celebrated stars in the repertory: Macaulay, and Thackeray, and others known to owners of five-foot bookshelves. These gentlemen have pictured Swift as a godless parson, a disappointed place-hunter, a political opportunist, a coarse bully, and a blackguard in his relations with women; ending his days in the solitude of his deanery at St. Patrick's Cathedral, Dublin, haunted by the terrors of madness, his body racked with pain. In short, a solemn example to us all of the dreadful retribution which is the due of those who presume to question the divine plan in Nature.

The decisive proof of his infamy has been seen in his three love affairs, none of which has met with the approval of posthumous critics, although at the time (so far as our evidence goes) no particular indignation or comment was excited by them. The first and briefest was with a young lady in the North of Ireland, whom he named Varina, and to whom he proposed marriage while he was the unhappy Rector of Kilroot, an Ulster parish full of Papists and Presbyterians, both equally obnoxious to Swift. Varina rejected him, but some years later, when he was appointed to a more substantial living, she wrote reminding him of her existence and suggesting that she was obviously designed to be his lawful spouse. He did not think so, and suggested that she was hardly fitted to be the wife of a poor parson. She accepted the suggestion and there ended Swift's first and only offer of marriage. He has received as little credit for it as for his subsequent failure to make such an offer in circumstances which have perplexed, fascinated, and irritated all his commentators ever since. In fact, so perverse are the ways of commentators that the very absence of all mention of marriage has impelled some of them to invent one. As there were two ladies in this later case, this invention has the double charm of making an honest woman of one, and of making Swift out to be a scoundrel towards the other, while proving that he could not have acted otherwise.

The situation arose out of his intimacy with Esther Johnson who had been, like himself, a protégée of Sir William Temple, and whom he had first met as a young man just over age while she was a child of six. Esther, having grown up into a very beautiful girl, received in her turn a classical name, Stella, and in that capacity she has become one of the heroines of English literature and almost of English fiction. She came to live in Dublin with her chaperon, and between these ladies and Swift there developed a relation which still defies the searchers after simple facts—since the absence of simplicity in facts is intolerable. Stella would not marry any of her worthy but obscure suitors and preferred to be the one great passion of Swift's life, the one intimate in his confidence and affections, rather than to lapse into the oblivion of a regular and respectable existence apart from him. The *Journal to Stella,* which records this *amitié amoureuse,* is a document unique in confessional literature, and so remarkable an account of the relations of a great man and an unusual woman that even Swift's fiercest detractors become sentimental over it and are kind enough to grant that the inventor of the "little language" in which they caressed each other was a human being. From that to assuming he was a married man was but a step.

The gossip and hearsay upon which this assumption is based will be found in most of the biographies and will supply the cynical with curious reading. Even the biographers who have too much sense to decide in favor of law and order adopt a non-committal attitude with the emphasis in that direction. This enables them all to raise cries of horror when Swift becomes entangled with the third lady to whom he lent a classical name, Vanessa. Vanessa was an intellectual young woman but, I regret to say, she had "a baby face," according to Swift, and a boyish form, and a third point in common with many of her successors to-day, a decided indifference to the ideals of Mr. Volstead.

JONATHAN SWIFT

Their friendship began in the usual way, but it soon developed in a way which is also not unusual, and their correspondence shows him alternately scolding and petting, humoring and flattering her, trying to satisfy her with intellectual friendship and to evade the obvious implications of her every word and attitude. In the poem "Cadenus and Vanessa" in which this philandering was recorded, Swift wrote:

> But what success Vanessa met,
> Is to the world a secret yet.
> Whether the nymph, to please her swain,
> Talks in a high romantick strain;
> Or whether he at last descends
> To act with less seraphick ends;
> Or, to compound the business, whether
> They temper love and books together;
> Must never to mankind be told,
> Nor shall the conscious muse unfold.

The lines very fairly reflect the actual situation, and Vanessa specifically absolves Swift from being responsible for the fact that the affair drifted beyond the limits which he had assigned to it. The melodramatists insist that Vanessa discovered Swift was married by writing to Stella and asking the question and that, as a result of a subsequent scene with Swift, she died of a broken heart. They regard this as a proper punishment for such unheard-of wickedness on the part of a married man.

There is every reason to suppose that the marriage was as apocryphal as the story of Vanessa's death. She, like Stella, seems to have preferred her relationship with Swift to all the comforts of a home, and every scrap of direct testimony from the ladies themselves runs contrary to the convenient theory. For some reason this attitude on the part of Stella and Vanessa is never considered, and Swift is blamed, first, for having offered to marry Varina and been refused; second, for not marrying Vanessa, when he is alleged to have been already married to Stella; third, for not acknowledging his marriage to Stella, thereby hastening her death. The only person who was confessedly unhappy was Vanessa, and her unhappiness, as she admitted, was due to the overpowering love which she had for Swift and his avowed inability to reciprocate it. Nevertheless a vast amount of indignation and pity has been aroused by the plight of Stella—immortalized in the *Journal* and contented, as she well might be, to be the closest friend and confidant of the most brilliant figure of his time.

An aspect of the case which Swift's innumerable censors have failed to consider is one which cannot but interest us, now that we are all psycho-analysts or psycho-analyzed. I refer to the deduction that

JONATHAN SWIFT

Swift's mother may not have really been his parent, and that Sir William Temple was very probably his father. The relations between Jonathan and his mother, to say the least of it, were unconventional. His nurse ran off with him from Dublin to England when he was one year old, and his mother left him there for three years, on the pretext that he could not stand the journey back. She was a "beautiful, but flighty and peculiar woman" and on one occasion, when she came to Dublin to see her son, she took lodgings and, after asking the landlady if she could keep a secret, informed the good woman that the rooms were for the purpose of "receiving the visits of a gallant," who was simply the Reverend Jonathan Swift, Rector of Laracor, near Dublin. It is further significant that when Jonathan was leaving college she should direct him to the care of Sir William Temple, an important personage, high in the councils of States, who made no demur but took the greatest interest in him and looked after him. A contemporary document, in *The Gentlemen's Magazine* of November, 1757—when Stella's mother was still alive and also Sir William Temple's heir—declared that Swift "was ignorant of his natural relation to Stella" and did not discover it until he proposed to marry her. Linking this with the scene, often related, of how Swift passed a friend coming out of the library of the Archbishop of Dublin, and how the Archbishop said, "you have just this moment passed the most miserable man on earth, but as to the cause of that misery you must never ask a question," one arrives at the conclusion that this was the occasion when Swift discovered that he and Stella were both the children of Sir William Temple. The article in an important and reputable magazine was not refuted when there were first-hand witnesses to do so, and we have the now illuminating statement in Swift's own words that "the only woman in the world who could make him happy, as a wife was the only woman in the world who could not be his wife." Emphasis upon the adverb "only" in the second clause of that sentence bring us to the point where we may ask if Swift did not precede Byron, with Stella in the place Augusta Leigh, but without a Harriet Beecher Stowe to air the scandal in a family periodical.

The irony of the protests against the ambiguity of Swift's relation to Stella, especially because of his failure to publish the banns, becomes, in the circumstances, a counterpart to the irony of the fate of *Gulliver's Travels*. Nowadays, for all our avidity for scandal, how easily our authors thrive on a tithe of the gossip, suspicion, and hostility which Swift and Stella aroused! I submit, with newspaper headlines in mind (true sign of greatness in this era of democracy), that Swift has claims upon the attention of the plain people. It is unfair of the professors to allow the general public to be fobbed off with "gift book" editions of one work, and to depict him as a foul-mouthed fellow who carried on with women as though he were an important movie star, but without sharing the latter's creditable enthusiasm for more and better marriage, and to deprive him of the pitiless publicity with which the aforesaid enthusiasm is associated. Instead, they shake their heads over the apparently unparallelled example of his unwillingness to marry, and hint at dark mysteries culminating in insanity—the advantage of this being that it can then be argued that the first two books, relating Gulliver's adventures among the Lilliputians and the Brobdingnagians, are charming, benign fantasies; humanity seen through the two ends of a telescope. But the third book, with the floating island of Laputa, where the imbecility of pedants is seen in all its glory, with Glubdubdrib, where the glorious dead are resurrected and reveal the absurdity of the true causes of their renown in the best Shavian style, with Luggnagg, where the Struldbrugs upset the romanticism of "Back to Methuselah"—the third book, it seems, marks the beginning of Swift's mental decline. As for the fourth, where we encounter the Houyhnhnms, the horses that are so superior to the humans, the Yahoos—it is dismissed as the filthy product of a diseased body and a diseased brain.

This notion of insanity has been widely used to discredit Swift, just as it has been charged, with a sneer, against Nietzsche that he died insane, the intention being to suggest that they need not, therefore, be taken too seriously. Yet even this point has never been so well established as to permit the assumptions based upon it. The medical testimony has favored the theory that Swift's disease was "not a case of gradually developing insanity, which might have affected his reason, even while its development was proceeding; but a case of specific malady, which tortured him during his life, and which ultimately produced a definite injury to the brain, but which up to that point in no way obliterated his reason." This disease—which has been analyzed by Oscar Wilde's father, Sir William Wilde, and many other physicians—eventually produced paralysis, and it was not until then that "the brain, already weakened by senile decay, at length gave way, and Swift sank into the dementia which preceded his death." In other words, here is a man who died at the age of seventy-eight, after years of ceaseless literary activity, as the nineteen volumes of his amazingly varied work testify; yet it is argued that his achievement is marked by insanity, although his literary activity ceased through old age and ill health for many years before his brain even began to be seriously affected.

What, it might naturally be asked, is the formidable character of Swift's work which renders necessary the insinuation that only one who was insane could have written it? Is it merely that it was in places obscene or disgusting? That has been alleged, especially in relation to *Gulliver's Travels,* but the more honest exegetists have frankly recognized that "the Augustans were free-spoken, and to a certain extent also foul-spoken," and it has not been argued that Sterne, Smollett, or John Cleland were mad. Indeed, one highly indignant but conscientious professor records that Swift's satire "in its broader aspect" was keenly relished. "The Queen and the Princess of Wales were in raptures over it. One noble lady facetiously identified herself with the Yahoos; another declared that her whole life had been lost in caressing the worst part of mankind, and in treating the best as her foes. And so surely could Swift rely on the most disgusting passages of his work being to the taste of the ladies of the Court, that in a private letter to one of the Maids of Honour he not only referred facetiously to one of its most indecent passages, but added to the indecency." From this we are to conclude that the moral degradation of the period was complete—not, if you please, that the eighteenth century had its conventions, and that it is as unreasonable to expect Swift to conform to any others as it would be to call a woman shameless to-day because she wears fewer and shorter clothes than her grandmother did.

In the absence of any such thing as an objective standard of obscenity, the application of moral tests to literature, without reference to the person concerned and the prevailing standards, usually leads to illogical and incoherent censorship. The bowdlerization of Swift may be counted, therefore, not as an effort to save us from the ravings of a lunatic but as one of the necessities of the false principle invoked, with the insinuation of madness thrown in as a makeweight to bolster up the case. Even the professional moralists do not pretend that the authors of books which offend their pruriency are insane. Swift must have committed a graver offence than "The Lady's Dressing Room" or "Strephon and Chloe" in an age which read Cleland's *Fanny Hill* and Mandeville's *Virgin Unmasked*—an age which might have subscribed to the lines which the author of "The Beggar's Opera" wrote for his own epitaph:

>Life is a jest: and all things show it.
>I thought so once, and now I know it.

JONATHAN SWIFT

To mention Gay and that charming piece—in which Swift is supposed to have had a hand—is to come at once to the fundamental objection to Swift, as he appears to his nineteenth-century censors: "the apostate politician, the ribald priest, the perjured lover, the heart burning with hatred against the whole human race," to quote the most celebrated summary of the indictment. The light paradoxes of "The Beggar's Opera" have annoyed very serious persons, but they are as superficial and harmless as the humor of a Gilbert and Sullivan opera. There is a topsy-turvy morality in this "Newgate pastoral" but its thrusts at society are as painless as the allusions to the House of Lords in "Iolanthe." Swift's satire is more destructive; it is, in fact, so deadly that successive generations have labored, as he would expect them to, in order by various devices to deflect his blows. He stands in the same relation to Gay and the other wits of his time as Bernard Shaw stands to Gilbert or to Oscar Wilde. England was enchanted by the happy melodies and playful fancy of Gilbert and Sullivan, and smiled at the epigrams of Oscar Wilde, but when the author of *Plays Pleasant and Unpleasant* turned that boasted "normal" vision of his upon the institutions and society around him, his gibes and mockery were resented.

It is interesting to compare these two Anglo-

Irish writers, who never lose an opportunity of reviling Ireland and of working rebelliously for her interests as against those of England. "His deficiency on the side of what we commonly call sentiment is not less remarkable. Sentiment is never likely to be found in any degree where the transcendental instinct is lacking. But the total atrophy, or rather non-existence, of both in a man of strong affections and of acute susceptibility to emotional impression is an anomaly rare indeed. . . . Its expression in language he regarded as cant, its expression in action as affectation and folly. For him life had no illusions, man no mystery, nature no charm. . . . His sole criterion as a critic and judge was unsublimated reason. . . . In his estimate of life and the world generally he saw everything in the clear cold light of the pure intellect. From no mind of which we have expression in record had the Spectres of the Tribe, the Den, the Forum, and the Theatre been so completely exorcised. But, as the eyes of the body may be blinded by excess of light, so the eyes of the mind may by excess of reason be blinded—by the very power that gives them sight." These words were written when Shaw was still the obscure Socialist author of "Widowers' Houses," and they occur in the last full-length study of Swift to appear in English. How often were they to be ap-

JONATHAN SWIFT

plied, with minor variations, to Shaw during the greater part of the following thirty years which witnessed his gradual rise to success and popularity. By a pleasant coincidence that popularity finally culminated in something akin to Swift's. The scourge and terror of the orthodox provides as good an evening's laughter in the theater as *Gulliver's Travels* in the nursery or drawing-room.

Bernard Shaw now amuses where he once horrified; but not so Swift, when his own ideas are presented as he conceived and expressed them. Swift had no faith or panacea; Shaw had, and it has proved his undoing, thereby absolving future professors from the task of making him obscure and inaccessible through expurgation and the thousand-and-one devices of pedantry for rendering literary virtue hateful. With an effort we now remember that Shaw labeled his work as Socialism, and delayed his reception at the hands of the general public until everybody was assured that the Home was not about to totter, and that the Servile State had no such charms with which to soothe the British breast as the Fabian Society pretended. His propaganda became obsolete long before his audience could be persuaded, and now he is confronted by a generation which is neither interested in nor frightened by what he offered as the constructive side of his philosophy. He is a skilled dramatic craftsman who can furnish an excellent show. His ideas are accepted in so far as they respond to the skepticism and iconoclasm of the times. We look to him for confirmation of our doubts, not for solutions to our insoluble problems.

As the greatest of doubters and iconoclasts in English, Swift is supreme, and it is in their flight from his merciless irony, his superb irreverence, and his magnificent contempt for the incurable imbecility of the human race that the orthodox have done everything possible to frustrate his influence. A dead rebel is usually a picturesque figure, just as pacifists in the ranks of one's enemy in wartime appear as truth-seeking idealists, entirely unlike the unpatriotic domestic product of the same kind. English literature has had many such romantic characters whose pleas for anarchy, free love, vegetarianism, communism, universal peace, and other similar abominations excite later idealists to deep enthusiasm and kindle a benign, almost tearful smile of understanding condescension in even the sternest academic pillars of society. Jonathan Swift gives no opportunity for this liberalism by proxy; he offers no chances for easy magnanimity. He is so much alive, so inescapable a menace to all the illusions and humbug essential to what we deem our happiness, that one may suppress him but he cannot be explained away. Hence that blessed word "insanity," which covers a multitude of cynicisms. Had he only advocated some dogma, however revolutionary, time would have proved it as futile as all things, and retrospective tolerance would have acquitted him of wickedness, if not of heresy, now fortunately harmless.

Swift's contribution to the literature of Utopias has nothing of the fervor of the Encyclopædists and those romantic inventors of the idea of Progress who, as another Dean, also accused of cynicism —Dean Inge—points out, enslaved three different philosophies to what is in the last analysis a question of statistics or, as I have said, plumbing and profits. The Houyhnhnms, not the Yahoos, are perfectible. Lemuel Gulliver, when he returns from his travels, finds no joy in seeing his wife and children again. He can only gradually accustom himself to the contact of his fellow-men, and when he at last resigns himself to the society of the usual lords, politicians, cut-throats, lawyers, and fools— he has for ever renounced all projects for the improvement of the Yahoos of the United Kingdom. The sarcasm of Voltaire, the sentimental apostrophes of Rousseau, the smiling skepticism of Montaigne are mild reformist platitudes beside the ruthless misanthropy of Swift, but there is an echo of him in the merciless last chapter of *Penguin Island,* where Anatole France's vision of the future is a not very inspiring point in that vicious circle known as the story of mankind.

Swift, then, committed the unpardonable sin of disbelieving in human perfectibility, and of expressing that disbelief in terms so memorable that timid souls are shocked and terrified by his reversal of Dante's descent into hell, for no stars are visible to restore hope to the soul. Like all pessimists he is charged by complacent optimists with reflecting his own personal misery and discontent, and of mistaking these for a picture of the world. That Swift was often unwell, and that, towards the end of his life, he was a very sick man (both physically and mentally) is as undeniable as the fact that the authors of glad fiction and manuals of right thought are frequently bilious. But nothing could be further from the truth than the idea that a disillusioned view of life is the mark of disappointment and personal unhappiness. There lives more joy in honest cynicism than in half the creeds for which hollow-eyed and gloomy fanatics die or struggle on behalf of progress. Swift once said that "the latter part of a wise man's life is taken up in curing the follies, prejudices, and false opinions he had contracted in the former," and the consequent adjustment of one's disbelief in human nature produces that happy equilibrium known as skepticism, which is erroneously believed to reflect discontent. One must lose a great number of illusions before existence, above the vegetable state, becomes tolerable. In the enormous range of Jonathan Swift's writings there is ample proof of this, and overwhelming evidence against the theory—so sedulously fostered—that he was a gloomy, morbid malcontent whose one moment of pleasant fancy was the composition of the Lilliput and Brobdingnag parts of *Gulliver's Travels*. The variety of his interests, the delightful irony of his humor, and the fertile wit and mischief of his subtle intellectual play, added to the famous Irish pamphlets—which have easily survived their immediate object, unlike most political pamphlets—are all a sufficient answer to his detractors. They show a man who up to the age of sixty years was incessantly active, alert, and stimulating, and who unostentatiously did more good of a practical kind than most romantic humanitarians brooding and weeping over the injustices of the world. He had no belief in the abstraction Justice, but the "Drapier's Letters" actually abolished the definite injustice of Wood's halfpence in Ireland. He had the greatest contempt for the plain people of Ireland, but his "Modest Proposal" remains to this day one of the greatest indictments of England's exploitation of them. If he left his fortune to found a Hospital for Lunatics and Incurables for the nation that needed it most, the tangible fact of his gift is not diminished by its being accompanied with a sardonic witticism rather than with a pious platitude.

The essays, pamphlets, letters, and occasional pieces of all kinds which are preserved in the collected editions of Swift's works are seldom seen by others than specialists, and the average reader must be content with an expurgated *Gulliver's Travels* and a nodding acquaintance with such writings as *A Tale of a Tub, The Battle of the Books,* and the *Journal to Stella.* It is upon that supposition that the legend of Swift has flourished, a legend well calculated to make most of us rely upon our childhood memories of Captain Gulliver to serve us all our lifetime. Yet, much that delights the heart of this unregenerate age has its counterpart in Swift, to a degree which encourages the belief that at no time since the close of his own age has there been an audience better fitted to appreciate him than now. The essay on "Polite Conversation," with its priceless dialogue, is as effective a record of inanity as the Discussion on Death in the *Book of Burlesques* of H. L. Mencken; it is an authentic "clinical note." On June the 20th, 1709, in *The Tatler,* Swift faced the now palpitating question in advanced circles: Can Men and Women be Friends? His advice to a common he-man, who complains, "it is my misfortune to be six feet and a half high, two full spans between the shoulders, thirteen inches diameter in the calves; and before I was in love, I had a noble stomach, and usually went to bed sober with two bottles"—his advice to this victim of the higher feminism has a flavor of *actualité*. "This order of Platonic ladies are to be dealt with in a manner peculiar from all the rest of the sex. Flattery is the general way, and the way in this case; but it is not to be done grossly. . . . A Platonne is not to be touched with panegyric: she will tell you, it is a sensuality in the soul to be delighted that way. You are not therefore to commend, but silently consent to all she does and says." The effect of this procedure having been illustrated, Swift concludes that "she will fall in with the necessities of mortal life, and condescend to look with pity upon an unhappy man, imprisoned in so much body, and urged by such violent desires."

There is the humor of a Gilbert and Sullivan libretto in the elaborate fooling of the "Scheme to make an Hospital for Incurables," with its schedule of the cost of maintaining incurable knaves, incurable scolds, incurable scribblers, incurable liars, and so forth: "incurable fools are almost infinite; however at first I would have only twenty thousand." Another typical piece of satire is the

"True Narrative" of how London behaved when it was believed that the end of the world had come, how "no less than one hundred and twenty-three clergymen" were ferried over to Lambeth to petition that a short prayer might be penned, as there was none in the service for such occasions, but "as in things of this nature it is necessary that the Council be consulted, their request was not immediately complied with." The whole town became seriously religious, but "all the different persuasions kept by themselves, for, as each thought the other would be damned, not one would join in prayer with the other." The grave irony of this is as irresistible as the conclusion of the argument against "The Abolishing of Christianity," wherein he says, "I do very much apprehend that, in six months' time after the act is passed for the extirpation of the gospel, the Bank and East India stock may fall at least one *per cent*. And since that is fifty times more than ever the wisdom of our age thought fit to venture for the preservation of Christianity, there is no reason we should be at so great a loss, merely for the sake of destroying it."

One has only to dip at haphazard into Swift's writings to realize that the picture of him as a malevolent hypochondriac rests on nothing more substantial than the common superstition that a skeptic must be abnormal and miserable. His

JONATHAN SWIFT

capacity for seeing himself in perspective does not even absolve him; and while it has been solemnly demonstrated that he was a good churchman, he is not credited with seeing the eternal humor of "a set of men suffered, much less employed and hired, to bawl one day in seven against the lawfulness of those methods most in use, toward the pursuit of greatness, riches, and pleasure, which are the constant practice of all men alive on the other six." His Latin epitaph upon himself is quoted with pitying concern, but it must be read in conjunction with the poem upon his death, in which he describes, with the most cynical good humor, how the news is received and credits his three best friends with remembering him for one month, one week, and one day respectively.

The horrible physical pain of his last years must excite pity, but Swift's life and achievement are above the cheap melodramatics with which they have been clothed. A great English critic, but naturally not a pedagogue, stands almost alone in his appropriate if brief treatment of Jonathan Swift. With an irony Swift would have admired, Hazlitt wrote, "There is nothing more likely to drive a man mad than the being unable to get rid of the idea of the distinction between right and wrong, and an obstinate, constitutional preference of the true to the agreeable." And he answered the sentimental moralists by saying, "nothing solid, nothing valuable is left in his system but virtue and wisdom. What a libel is this upon mankind!" Swift was the embodiment of his age, and it was an age which, as a whole, found itself subjected in some degree to the same reproaches as he—which may be summed up in the word materialism. The Augustans were not, we are told, idealists; they had none of the exaltations, romantic and revolutionary, which possessed the eighteenth century at its close. By that time the illusion of progress had become so well fixed in certain minds that to suggest doubts as to the beneficent results of the French Revolution was to incur the anathema of the millennium-makers.

Nowadays we can measure exactly how beautifully that Revolution and all its accompanying cant served the spread, not of liberty, but of industrialism and that form of democracy which is the negation of the only kind of freedom that is conceivable—that which fosters the development of intelligent individuals. "Some men," said Swift, "admire republics, because orators flourish there, and are the greatest enemies of tyranny; but my opinion is that one tyrant is better than a hundred." The day of the rabble was approaching, and Swift described the Yahoos. In the dark years of his slow death an ardent youth from Switzerland named Rousseau made his appearance in Paris, preparing a message on Equality, to which Swift's posthumous "Directions to Servants" reads like a grimly ironical retort. He once assessed the number of superior persons in Britain at twenty-five, and at one thousand those "who have a tolerable share of reading and good sense." The estimate is a little over-generous, but let it stand, for it represents the audience to which Jonathan Swift addressed himself and to which he will always appeal: the happy few whose happiness consists in accepting the ironies of life and rejecting its illusions.

Chapter Five

LORD BYRON

THE fame of Lord Byron, unlike that of his predecessors in this volume, is not consecrated and unchallenged. He has not been dead long enough to satisfy the professors, who require more than a hundred years in which to make up their minds. The centenary of his death in 1924 was appropriately marked by what was the third failure to obtain his admission to the company of the great in Westminster Abbey. When this project was first attempted, in 1824, the respected presence of Walter Scott on the Memorial Committee did not soften the hearts of the Dean and Chapter, nor unloosen enough purse-strings to provide compensation for a British sculptor. It was a mere foreigner, therefore, the great Danish sculptor Thorwaldsen, who made the statue which lay for ten years in the customs while fruitless efforts were made to present it to the British nation. It finally found shelter in the Library of Trinity College, Cambridge, because, as a reverend bishop cogently remarked, "if Lord Byron in his works attacked the founder of our Religion, and, by the beauties of his verse was one of the most dangerous advisers of youth, his statue does not deserve a place in the Temple of our God." A suggestive commentary upon this failure of our orthodox and academic leaders to admit Byron unreservedly into the fold is the fact that he is the only English author, with the possible exception of Shakespeare, whose fame is both popular and universal. He has an advantage over the Bard, in being actually known and read where professorial writs do not run, and he has exerted an influence outside his own country, upon both the intellectuals and the plain people, such as no British predecessor, contemporary, or successor can claim. Hence, I suspect his precarious but indubitable presence in the literary manuals, which are reluctant to surrender a glory so tangible, if thoroughly reprehensible from every conventional standpoint. Ever since Byron first horrified the quarterly reviewers, the mandarins have looked askance at this disturbing phenomenon, fluctuating in their attitude to such a degree that the story has been chronicled in a stout volume, obviously out of all proportion to Byron's importance as a poet. Nothing, in fact, could better illustrate the futility of all the grave talk about "standards," "values," and "significance" on the part of the trustees of tradition, than this inability to admit once and for all that Byron was an inconsiderable poet, and that the courage of their convictions demands his immediate dismissal.

During his lifetime Byron thoroughly enjoyed flouting every convention and upsetting the equanimity of all humbugs. It is consoling to know that his posthumous effect is just what he would have desired. He is still the scourge of the timorously respectable who want to eat their literary cake and have it, and his treatment by the spokesmen of posterity is a beautiful study in the art of squirming and wriggling. If they would only stick to their business as appraisers of dead literature, his unhappy victims could escape with some show of logic and dignity. But Byron defied them by establishing his reputation over their heads, and as he, "being dead yet speaketh," there is nothing to be done but grin and bear him, always in the secret hope that another hundred years may see the end of him.

There is something symbolical, as well as ironically characteristic of Byron's literary fate in the circumstances which attended the publication of his first book, the rare quarto known as *Fugitive Pieces*. The whole edition was burned at the instance of the Rev. John Becher, who objected to the wickedness of the verses "To Mary," save two copies, his own, from which the offending pages

LORD BYRON

were torn, and one other, whose existence enables us to measure the extent of the young poet's depravity. As this poem appears in none of the standard editions of Byron's works, a few verses may be quoted. They are the first manifestation of Byronism:

> Though love than ours could ne'er be truer,
> Yet flames too fierce themselves destroy,
> Embraces oft repeated cloy,
> *Ours* came too *frequent* to endure.
>
> Even now I cannot well forget thee,
> And though no more in folds of pleasure
> Kiss follows kiss in countless measure,
> I hope *you* sometimes will regret me.
>
> And smile to think how oft were done,
> What prudes declare a sin to act is,
> And never but in darkness practice,
> Fearing to trust the tell-tale sun.
>
> And wisely therefore night prefer,
> Whose dusky mantle veils their fears,
> Of *this,* and *that,* of eyes and ears,
> Affording shades to those that err.
>
> Now, by my soul, 'tis most delight
> To view each other panting, dying,
> In love's *ecstatic posture* lying,
> Grateful to *feeling,* as to *sight.*

LITERARY BLASPHEMIES

And had the glaring God of Day
(As formerly of Mars and Venus)
Divulg'd the joys which pass'd between us,
Regardless of his *peeping* ray,

Of love admiring such a *sample,*
The Gods and Goddesses descending,
Had never fancied us offending,
But *wisely* followed *our example.*

When Lord Byron was born, just one year before the French Revolution, the eighteenth century was being violently precipitated into the dreadful era of political democracy and statistical progress. By the time he began to write, England was in the midst of an anti-revolutionary hysteria comparable to that in which Europe and America lapsed after the war and the Bolshevik victory in Russia. Fear of the French Revolution and fear of Napoleon, whose retreat from Moscow coincided with the appearance of "Childe Harold" in 1812, created an atmosphere in which the same elements were present as have plagued us ever since 1914. The literary world was also in a plight analogous to that in which it has found itself during the last decade. While the authorities were panic-stricken, the intellectuals were divided into those who had been disillusioned by the failure of the millennium to materialize, and those who had vague hopes that somewhere, somehow the Good, the True, and the

LORD BYRON

Beautiful were about to be vindicated. The result of this disenchanted state of mind was a period, like all periods of transition, when the ardors of yesterday were dead and acquiescence in accomplished facts had not yet established the new equilibrium, which was to come a few years after Byron's death, when "the stupid nineteenth century," as a French critic has called it, got into its ponderous stride.

Byron, therefore, was a typical product of the Regency, of an age like our own, when the current nostrums were rapidly losing their effectiveness and the horizon was being scanned for a new panacea. The disillusionment with libertarian catchwords was then, of course, somewhat slower than it has recently become. The French Revolution had still an air of novelty, and political liberty had a glamour with which no rational human being can invest it to-day. Consequently, while he obviously had no illusions about mankind, Byron employed the rhetoric of revolutionary romance so effectively that he at once became, and remains to this day, an object of veneration to confiding souls who imagine that what was good enough for Rousseau must be good enough for them. He is respected in radical circles as the poet of rebellion, and since there is no rebel like a dead rebel, even the conservative are inclined to point with a certain pride to this English aristocrat's stand for Liberty. Having done all that was humanly possible to stem the forces of revolution in Europe during the last years of the eighteenth century, England has the retrospective pleasure of recalling how nobly Coleridge, Shelley, Keats, and Wordsworth sang of Freedom. As a typical representative of this devotion to safely remote revolutionary movements has said, this poetic passion for liberty is essential to the self-respect of the English-speaking world. "Otherwise, whatever success may attend on Democracy or on Empire, the Anglo-Saxon race will have failed in its mission of spreading in widest commonalty the highest pleasures which the human spirit can enjoy."

Byron, to do him justice, understood perfectly this peculiar temperament of his countrymen, as his letters show. "As to the estimation of the English which you talk of, let them calculate what it is worth before they insult me with their insolent condescension. I have not written for their pleasure. If they are pleased, it is that they chose to be so; I have never flattered their opinions, nor their pride; nor will I." And so while his services on behalf of rebellion were a source of national satisfaction to the sentimental liberals of posterity, his contemporaries described him as "impiously railing against his God—madly and meanly dis-

LORD BYRON

loyal to his Sovereign and his country—and brutally outraging all the best feelings of family honour, affection and confidence." References to the "bravo's trade" in "Childe Harold" arouse his critics to ask, "not without some anxiety and alarm, whether such are indeed the opinions which a British peer entertains of a British army," and the "calm, careless ferociousness of contented and satisfied depravity" is regarded as his outstanding achievement and characteristic as a poet. He is not "such a poet as virgins might read, and Christians praise, and Englishmen take pride in." The fact that all three consummations have been witnessed since Byron's death is, I think, one of the pleasantest ironies of literary history as taught in classrooms.

His popularity in his own day, as these diatribes might suggest, was enormous. His publisher declared that in ten years Byron's pen had brought in $375,000, and the sale of 14,000 copies of one of his books in a single day is recorded. All this proceeded while scandals raged about him, while his publishers refused to print his work unless they censored it, and while a panic-stricken government could not persuade itself that, after the defeat of Waterloo, England's bogey, Napoleon, no longer required the vigilance which had filled the country with the coercive measures and spies once more associated in our minds with crusades for liberty and democracy. Byron had separated from his wife and gone to live on the Continent, where he found in wine—or to be precise, gin—women, and revolutionary songs an outlet for his rebellious energies. While his own people were gradually approaching the Nirvana of bourgeois industrialism, Byron was declaiming against throne, home, and altar, and aiding the propaganda of ideas which had ceased to enchant English ears. But he was not happy; both his health and his amours and the prolonged society of certain radical friends who were "fighting for the Cause" drove him into the one great adventure of his career. He set out for Greece to take part in the Greek War of Independence. As one of his few intelligent biographers has said: "Lord Byron accomplished nothing at Missolonghi except his own suicide: but by that single act of heroism he secured the liberation of Greece."

When he died at the age of thirty-six, England was almost ripe for the reaction which set in against him. A few years later the Reform Bill proved that the lesson of feeding the political dog with its own tail was the one tangible product of the Revolution. Political reform, it turned out, was the nostrum required to keep the rabblement and its leaders busy for a few generations. The middle classes emerged under this benign dispensation, and evangelical Christianity went hand in hand with profits. Victorianism set in with all its severity and the heresies of Byron ceased to delight a generation that demanded the pious platitudes of a Tennyson. By the middle of the nineteenth century the reputation of the author of "Don Juan" was eclipsed. He had been relegated to the limbo of the unrighteous and his intrinsic qualities were not such as could stand comparison with those of his younger contemporaries, Keats and Shelley. They, at least, were poets of that lineage which never dies so long as there are men and women sensitive to melody and color. The mystery is how did this judgment of the age to which the professors by definition and predilection belong come to be reversed? By what freak of nature did this exotic bird find a perch among the decorous domestic fowl of our "standard authors"?

To an eminent American Victorian must be given the credit for that remarkable achievement. In 1869 Mrs. Harriet Beecher Stowe enlivened simultaneously the pages of a decorous magazine in Boston and London with an article entitled "The True Story of Lady Byron's Married Life." The following year this was expanded into a volume, *Lady Byron Vindicated: a History of the Byron Controversy*. The Byron controversy was not, at that time, a discussion as to the literary merits of Byron, but an exchange of opinions, conjectures, gossip, and slander concerning the separation of Lord and Lady Byron and the reasons which had sent the poet into exile. Both parties to the separation had partisans, but, on the whole, opinion sympathised with him rather than with his wife, who was abused and misrepresented incredibly. Mrs. Stowe, having done so much for Uncle Tom, decided to do something for Lady Byron, who had taken the American novelist into her confidence. So she dropped her stone into the literary frog-pond, to no inconsiderable effect. She informed all and sundry that Byron had been guilty of incest with his half-sister, Augusta Leigh, and that this was the reason why Lady Byron and her husband parted. It was Mrs. Stowe's ingenuous belief that this revelation would not only vindicate her friend, but destroy once and for all the influence and prestige of Byron.

I need hardly say that Mrs. Stowe's article and book enormously increased the sale of Byron's works. By provoking endless replies, confirmations, counter-arguments, and lampoons she revived an interest in him which was no less vehement than that which prevailed during his life. What was then the talk of a limited circle was now the sensation of two continents. Byron's relations with Augusta were but a part of the scandal that accompanied him while he lived, and they did not seem more than usually wicked in a man whose family records read like an extract from the Newgate calendar, as one of his biographers has remarked: "While respectable folk refused to believe their ears, but opened them wide, the legal representatives of Lady Byron merely declared that Mrs. Stowe's story was not completely accurate and authoritative." But Byron's grandson, the Earl of Lovelace, being less legalistic in his phraseology, allowed "that Mrs. Stowe's statement is substantially correct." As has since been demonstrated, her offense lay, not in the charge against Byron, but in her betrayal of a confidence ten years before Lady Byron had authorized the publication of the truth. Furthermore, her narrative was incomplete, incoherent, and disingenuous.

Needless to say, while the Byron revival flourished on this scandal, the most strenuous efforts were made to evade the vital fact, and to this day the evidence, overwhelming as it has since become, merely causes the orthodox to shudder. The biographers of Byron who faced the evidence realistically are those outside the academic world. Byron's grandson, in 1905, was at last free to publish the essential documents, and these have been accepted by intelligent critics and biographers as beyond dispute. We now know that Mrs. Stowe was right when she said that Byron and his sister were lovers, and the parents of the strange child Medora, whose own story added to the blaze of controversy after the Stowe revelations. But we also know that incest was not the cause of the separation of the Byrons, for Lady Byron believed that her husband and Augusta had broken off their relationship when he married. She and Augusta were friends, and all the impassioned correspondence from Byron to his sister, reproaching her with her newly found virtue and declaring his undying love for her, seems to have been shown by Augusta to his wife, who helped her to resist him.

Lord Lovelace's documentary statement of the case introduces letters which absolutely confirm what were previously well-founded but unproven conjectures. These letters, when coupled with the poems inspired by the same circumstances, the "Epistle to Augusta," the third canto of "Childe Harold," "Stanzas to Augusta," and the famous poem beginning

I speak not—I trace not—I breathe not thy name—
There is love in the sound—there is Guilt in the fame—

fail to convince the pedagogues, the most recent of whom declare that "there is not a line in them capable of being perverted by the most unhealthy

LORD BYRON

imagination into evidence against Byron and Mrs. Leigh." The professor excepts one sentence, an allusion to Lucretia Borgia, the implications of which are obvious, but does not trouble to account for this peculiar allusion. He evades the first volume of Lord Byron's correspondence by calling it "unpleasant," and recommending a judicial attitude of suspended judgment, in the face of facts which are as clearly established as such facts could possibly be, that is by original documents and the statements of all parties directly concerned.

This phase of Byron's reputation and the position adopted towards it by the schoolmen, it will be seen, is not without its humor. The life and character of Byron are obviously what hold and fascinate, and the revival of interest in him produced by the further evidence concerning his life has given him a new lease of academic fame, yet in those very circles upon which popular opinion has again thrust him, an obstinate effort is still made to deny the central fact of his life. Yet nothing is more apparent than the manner in which Byron the poet depended entirely upon the glamour of Byron the man, who was Byron the rake, the daredevil, the rebel. The rise and fall of his fame have been meticulously recorded, and the slump which followed his death has been variously explained. But the connection between the revival of Byron and the revival of his own story is inescapable. The learned commentators shrink from this conclusion, and while they profess their profound admiration for the champion of freedom and deprecate all allusions to his immorality, one of them actually cites Mrs. Humphry Ward and George Moore as examples of depravity comparable to his.

Those who have been taught to recoil in horror from the "immorality" of James Joyce's *Ulysses,* and who observe the stern disapprobation with which their mentors regard the ingenuous outpourings of contemporary radicals with views on love and Freud and single tax, may rightly wonder how Byron enjoys their favor. His love-affairs show him to be the first of the English literary exhibitionists, and his love for Augusta, although dramatized in the best Byronic manner in "Manfred" and the "Bride of Abydos," seems to have been privately a matter of intense satisfaction to him and the only love in his life that ever stirred him deeply. He was impenitent, therefore, to a degree which surpasses the mild defiance of moral conventions in which the most unpardonable of the moderns has ever indulged. The chronicle of his amours, apart from this special case, is sufficient to cause his banishment by every right-thinking library committee in these States.

His religious and political heresies, in fact,

would alone insure refusal to admit him to these hospitable shores. He conspired with the Carbonari of Italy and he made the independence of Greece possible. Like Gorky, he was not the sort of man that an esteemed American novelist could associate with—in public, at least. Nevertheless, he has been temporarily admitted into the hall of fame. Is it any wonder that, in the process of arranging this, the guardians of the portals have got somewhat tangled up in their own regulations?

On the other hand, granted that they are, as usual, temporizing and trying to adapt themselves to what appear to be accomplished facts, what of his claims so eagerly granted by the advanced thinkers? Here is one of that ardent company— one of the most ardent—congratulating himself that "fortunately not all the poets of England let themselves be frightened by the French Revolution." Byron, it seems, was "the first lord of letters of that age and of all the ages"; no other "high-up aristocrat" achieved such greatness. He wrote in "Don Juan" "a hateful picture of a hateful world, but . . . we recognize in it a great spirit trying to lift itself above an age of corruption by the instrument of scorn." Shelley was "the best influence that ever came into his life," yet, as we know from a less romantic source, he refused to help the "Snake," as Shelley was called. "If we puffed the

Snake, it might not turn out a profitable investment. All trades have their mysteries. If we crack up a popular author, he repays us in the same coin, principal and interest—if we introduce Shelley to our readers, they might draw comparisons, and they are odious!" The comradeship of literary radicalism endureth forever.

However, such sentiments in a literary gent are not incompatible with the utmost zeal for the welfare of mankind as an abstraction. "Byron," says Upton Sinclair, "had now become the voice of liberty against reaction throughout Europe. . . . In the beginning he had written to amuse himself and his readers; he had catered to their sentimentalism and their folly. But in the end he came to despise his readers and wrote only to shock them. They had made a world of lies; and one man would tell them the truth. That is why to-day we rank him as a world force in the history of letters. . . . We are interested in a poet who possessed a clear eye and a clear brain, who saw the truth, and spoke it to all Europe, and helped to set free the future of the race. . . ."

This quotation is the most recent version of Byron, the idol of radicalism. It is a simplification of the man and is as irreconcilable with the truth as all the theories which attempt to divorce his public from his private utterances. A more

LORD BYRON

aristocratic English commentator once said that Byron "understood the rights of man, but he seems never to have heard of the rights of woman." This is another way of saying that he was unregenerate, for feminism, amongst his own associates, was already a dogma. Mary Wollstonecraft's *Rights of Women* had set the model for all subsequent dithyrambs against this man-made world.

Byron's practice with women had led him to conclusions which may be guessed by his statement that he gave his heroines "extreme refinement, joined to great simplicity and want of education." To Lady Blessington he remarked, "I have not quite made up my mind that women have souls," and he confessed that no more intelligence was desirable in a woman than "enough to be able to understand and value mine, but not sufficient to be able to shine herself. All men with pretensions desire this; though few, if any, have courage to avow it." On the only occasion when he considered himself bound by the past favors bestowed upon him by a lady, his reasons were clear but unsuggestive of democracy. "As neither her birth, nor her rank, nor connections of birth or marriage are inferior to my own, I am in honour bound to support her through." The truth is that Byron's philosophy of life had nothing of the revolutionary in it; he was rather the first of the "aristocratic radicals," in the sense of the term applied by Georg Brandes to Nietzsche. He did not sing of liberty, to quote the Danish critic, as "a thing which we can grasp with our hands, or confer as a gift in a constitution, or inscribe among the articles of a state church," but he uttered "the eternal cry of the human spirit, its never-ending requirement of itself."

His connection with revolutionary movements on the continent of Europe can be traced to his general restlessness and boredom and not to any conviction that principles were at stake. In the liberation of Italy he saw poetry become action, not the social, political, and economic problems involved. He admired Napoleon as an expression of the supremacy of the individual will, to the embarrassment of those who have tried to number Byron amongst the apostles of social revolution. He idealized revolt for revolt's sake, and his giaours, pirates, Laras, Manfreds, and Zuleikas are as incongruous in the temple of modern radicalism as Byron himself is amongst the household and schoolroom gods of England America. His part in popular movements of political emancipation was not that of the crusader, for he had no faith in the people, nor, at bottom, any hope for the future—his opinion of the Greeks for whom he is alleged to have died was skeptical and contemptuous to the last. "I need say little on that subject, I was a fool to come here; but, being here, I must see what is to be done," he wrote to Teresa Guiccioli. And again: "of the Greeks I can't say much good hitherto, and I do not like to speak ill of them, though they do of one another." He declared that if the authorities "were to set a pretty woman, or a clever woman, about me," his devotion to Greek independence might be diverted.

That is typical of the complete honesty, and the sense of the realities of his own character which Byron maintained in spite of cautious or romantically enthusiastic admirers and friends. He could never be persuaded to strike an attitude appropriate to the illusions of the various people who tried, and still try, to fit him into their own particular little scheme of things. When he sent the first part of "Don Juan" to his publishers, all his friends unanimously advised the suppression of the poem. But he was disposed to listen only for a short while. When the conviction finally took hold of him that he had written something of which he was sure, something that must stand, he delivered himself in terms which are curiously applicable to the subsequent attitude of the orthodox critics towards his work. "We will circumvent your cursed puritanical committee on that point in the end. . . . If they had told me the poetry was bad, I would have acquiesced; but they say the contrary, and then talk to me about morality." In another letter he said to his publisher: "You shan't make *canticles* of my cantos. The poem will please if it is lively; if it is stupid it will fail; but I will have none of your damned cutting and slashing. . . . I know the precise worth of popular applause, for few scribblers have had more of it; and if I choose to swerve into their paths, I could retain it, or resume it." His position is expressed—more Byronically —in the lines

> I could not tame my nature down; for he
> Must serve who fain would sway—and soothe—and sue—
> And watch all time—and pry into all places—
> And be a living lie—who would become
> A mighty thing among the mean, and such
> The mass are; I disdain'd to mingle with
> A herd, though to be leader—and of wolves. . . .

These characteristic sentiments are hardly those which we associate with a savior of mankind, although they correspond closely to the disillusioned individualism of the present day. It is not for nothing that a great French critic has suggested —though not in order to compliment either of them—that there is an analogy between the style of Swift and that of Byron. In both he sees "a disease of heart and mind," which is merely the inevitable formula for minimizing cynicism and skepticism, as we have seen in the analysis of Jonathan Swift's reputation. Byron emotionally sums up the philosophy of an age of transition like our own and consequently his work, if little read, presents curious parallels to that element in contemporary life and literature which causes disquietude to the sedate:

> I hope it is no crime
> To laugh at *all* things. For I wish to know
> *What,* after all, are *all* things—but a show?

These lines from "Don Juan" are like the retort of the younger generation to-day when sermonized by its shocked elders, and they are the epitome of the poem in which Byron expressed his whole being, saying that there was ten times as much truth in it, but that its lack of sentiment would make it unacceptable to those who needed illusions. Haidee, who "spoke not of scruples, ask'd no vows, nor offered any" also strikes us as having an appositeness to present circumstances over which much indignation has been expended. The epigraph of much modern American fiction is contained in

> Alas! They were so young, so beautiful,
> So lonely, loving, helpless, and the hour
> Was that in which the heart is always full,
> And, having o'er itself no further power,
> Prompts deeds eternity cannot annul.

Such an apologia would not nowadays bring down upon its author the charges of suborning youth which once were leveled against him. I rather suspect that eternity is now credited with powers of annulment beyond those with which Byron could publicly admit. Indeed, I fear that not even the professional moralists, with the worst intentions in the world, have been able, by suppression, to endow "Don Juan" with that surreptitious popularity which still sends the ingenuous in search of Boccaccio, Mlle. de Maupin, and the works of Rabelais.

Byron's romanticism is an obstacle to his appreciation in this jazz age, although his general point of view is similar, for similar reasons. As one of his most sincere critics said in a lecture at Princeton University—though himself an alien visitor there—"he hated and despised the spent forces, or what seemed to be such, on the side of conservation. To the last he was haunted by the ghosts of traditional beliefs, which had ceased to live within him as vital powers. He was a democrat among aristocrats and an aristocrat among democrats; a skeptic among believers and a believer among skeptics. . . . To his quick sense of humor more than to anything else he owed the sanity which controls or modifies his perturbations of mind." That summary very well describes the state of mind in the world to-day which is referred to in press and pulpit as the revolt of the younger generation. This, too, in Professor Dowden's phrase, is "an age of dissonance," and we resemble Byron, who "could not satisfy his hunger for life with abstract doctrines; he could not subsist on ideal hopes and faith; he had a great capacity for pleasure, a strong turn for reality. . . . No organized body of belief guided his intellect; no system of social duties controlled his heart; . . . what was old had lost its authority; what was new had not fully justified itself." All this emerges clearly from his poetry, but who can read it without an effort?

Certainly not the decorous gentlemen who try to persuade us that Byron is a great classic. The slightest examination of his work at once reveals the impossibility of its being acceptable to the pillars of society. The cant which was provoked by his personal life was bad enough, in all conscience, but the hypocrisy involved in bolstering up his literary reputation is even worse. The whitewashing of Shakespeare is nothing compared to it, for one can understand the effort to reconcile a poet of great genius with the evangelical conscience. It is so palpably disingenuous that neither the true story of Byron and Augusta Leigh, nor that of his Greek adventure, has had the slightest effect. His death at Missolonghi was suicide, his last desperate encounter with an ironical Destiny, but it serves as an admirable epilogue to the rake's career. The handbooks still refer to it as the redemption of a life of dissipation, and ignore the fact that he had previously contemplated exile to Venezuela and did not leave Italy until his existence there had been rendered intolerable.

When Mrs. Stowe set out so bravely to obliterate Byron from the records of respectable literary society, she underestimated the pusillanimity of the living toward the dead. The theories which have been brought forward, without a scrap of evidence, to counter the documentary proofs furnished by Byron's grandson in support of the incest charge are in themselves a study of the marvelous workings of the human mind. One writer actually argues that Augusta Leigh assumed the guilt in order to shield a woman whom she hardly knew from the accusation of adultery! The conservative critics have unanimously clutched at the wildest straws rather than accept the statements of Lord Lovelace who has convinced all biographers and commentators, without preconceived notions, from Sir Leslie Stephen to Miss Ethel Mayne. One would think, to watch these wrigglings, that Lord Byron's life, apart from his half-sister, had been such a theme for classroom eloquence that his love for Augusta would just break the professors'

LORD BYRON

hearts! Judged by their usual standards in such matters, they have already swallowed so many gnats in Byron's case that this particular camel ought not to be so difficult, especially as both the woman and himself were as frank about it as the parties in all Byron's other love affairs.

My own suspicion is that this determination to admit the prodigal son at all costs must be regarded as a subconscious manifestation of a peculiar dispensation of Providence to the Anglo-Saxon race. England is the country whose great artists and striking personalities deviate more markedly from the norm than in any other. They are sports of nature rather than the quintessence of all the qualities that go to make up the national character. In every Frenchman there is a Montaigne or a Pascal, but what had Shakespeare or Keats or Shelley in them of the characteristics associated in all minds with the typical Englishman? The solidity? The practical sense? The capacity for self-discipline? Assuming, therefore, as these arbiters of tradition have apparently assumed, that Byron is to be classed as one of England's wayward sons, a freak, a departure from the sacred rules of "good form"—in brief, an Englishman of genius—it becomes clear that concessions must be made, but not too many. Hence the gnats, but the rejection of the camel. Byron, if a great poet, had inevitably to be classified with "the poets of rebellion"—Wordsworth, Coleridge, Shelley, and Keats—who wrote during the French Revolutionary period, when Europe was inventing its new nostrum for human ills. Consequently, with a few clear-headed exceptions, the commentators have over-emphasized the element of revolt in his work in order to confuse his aspirations with those of the period. The radicals gladly annex a lord, and the conservatives love a well-connected revolutionary, when he is dead. It is very much as if one were to deduce from H. L. Mencken's attacks on Messrs Palmer and Burleson that he was a subscriber to the teachings of the I. W. W.

There is method, however, in this seeming madness on the part of British conservatism, for the Englishman of genius fulfills a very practical function, unknown to himself, I admit. He is to the nation what the incessant patter is to the conjuror; it diverts the attention of the audience from the trick. While we all think with moist eyes of the lovely way the English poets sang about liberty and brotherhood, our attention is distracted from the more tangible fact that it was the governing class in England, assisted, I need hardly say, by that good Irishman, Mr. Burke, which stemmed and broke the movement launched from Paris in the direction of that very freedom hymned by the poets. In our own day we are familiar with the English knight-errant who speaks only Irish in Ireland and urges the natives to die for their motherland and independence; with the liberty-loving liberal of good family, who has forsaken the comforts and traditions of his caste, in order to preach the gospel of democracy in . . . other countries. These are the gentlemen who do the talking while England proceeds with the serious business on hand. In countries where people are susceptible to ideas, this breed of genial eccentrics is unknown.

The fame of Lord Byron in Europe is bound up with that tradition of English eccentricity, and *Milord* summed up every superstition of the Continent concerning the Island Race. He personified the conception of her poets, and the image cherished in foreign revolutionary circles until the recent war for democracy, of an England ever ready to champion the oppressed. Being unaccustomed to measuring artists by their virtues as husbands, fathers, and taxpayers, continental critics were not disturbed by the carnalities and impieties of Byron's life and work. Moreover, the enchantment of distance lends a charm to Byron's verse which it lacks for those whose native tongue is English, and who are bound to compare him with authentic masters of that speech. The professorial euphemism has it that the poetry of Byron does not lend itself to selection, which means, in plain language, that the anthologists have difficulty in making his greatness plausible. In one of the standard English anthologies he is given six pages as against from three to five times as many for his contemporaries, Wordsworth, Coleridge, Shelley and Keats. One of the poems selected shows him at his best:

>So we'll go no more a-roving,
>   So late into the night,
>Though the heart be still as loving,
>   And the moon be still as bright.
>
>For the sword outwears its sheath,
>   And the soul wears out the breast,
>And the heart must pause to breathe,
>   And love itself have rest.
>
>Though the night was made for loving,
>   And the day returns too soon,
>Yet we'll go no more a-roving
>   By the light of the moon.

It is hardly necessary to point out that, delicate as this much-admired little poem is, it is neither great poetry nor the kind of poetry for which Byron is remembered, either by his detractors, by his admirers, or by his whitewashers. Many of our own contemporaries, about whom we have no

LORD BYRON

illusions of immortality, reach that level in the monthly magazines and are pilloried by fierce-eyed æsthetes for their old-fashioned sentimentality. Byron's actual life is an essential gloss upon his poetic professions, and was more truly expressed in

> Let us have wine and women, mirth and laughter,
> Sermons and soda-water the day after.
> Man, being reasonable, must get drunk;
> The best of life is but intoxication. . . .

If any lingering curiosity survives from our school days, it will be better satisfied by the study of Byron's own fascinating and turbulent life, which has at last been presented in focus, than by attempting to pump up enthusiasm for his Romantic rhetoric or horror at his supposed audacities. He was a personality, though not a poet, of our own "age of dissonance," and it is that dissonance in him which has its echo in the modern reader. To admit this is to give him the immortality which he deserves rather than the fame of which he wrote, with his usual contempt for self-deception,

> What is the end of Fame? 'tis but to fill
> A certain portion of uncertain paper. . . .
> For this men write, speak, preach, and heroes fall,
> And bards burn what they call their "midnight taper,"
> To have, when the original is dust,
> A name, a wretched picture, and worse bust.

Chapter Six

CHARLES DICKENS

THE reputation of Charles Dickens differs in one vital respect from that of the other classical writers whom I have considered: his fame is essentially popular. He is not an author whom the critics of his time had to defend against an indifferent public opinion, and his after-fame is not swathed in the mummy wrappings of academic annotators. The consequence is that, although the literature which has accumulated about him is voluminous, it lacks the unconscious humor of the customary classical exegetists, who have had no opportunity for the display of their peculiar talents. They have placed him on no pedestal like that of Shakespeare; they have not embalmed him like Milton; unlike Swift, he has not frightened them into misrepresentation; unlike Byron, he provides no horrified thrills which induce a determination to hush things up. His name is in all the college manuals and is familiar wherever books are read, but it owes nothing of its survival to professors, who, it is interesting to note, are but scantily represented in the bibliography of his commentators. Dickens is the first great author whom the plain people discovered for themselves.

When Charles Dickens was born, in 1812, the last flickering lights of the eighteenth century were disappearing, the nineteenth century in all its fatuity had rapidly set in, and by the time he had got over his literary nonage in *Sketches by Boz,* Queen Victoria was on the throne, and it already seemed as if what we know as Victorianism was an eternal and immutable condition. The superstition of progress and the dogma of democratic infallibility were enthroned, and an era had opened up which needed prophets of a character appropriate to its peculiar needs. Literature had ceased, or was ceasing, to be the possession of a civilized minority, and after various hesitations fiction emerged as the dominant literary *genre,* the form most suited to the mass consumption which became the result of the spread of "education." Most of the novelists who shared with Dickens the enthusiasm of this new public, Harrison Ainsworth, G. P. R. James, Theodore Hook, and Wilkie Collins, were so bad that by comparison Dickens seems more than great enough to explain his survival. If the others are now forgotten, we must not forget that to the taste which Dickens fostered they were as acceptable as he, for discrimination is no part of the demand out of which his fame grew.

With the possible exception of Walter Scott, whom "no adult can read and every grown-up person has read," as Georg Brandes remarks, Charles Dickens represents the beginning of that species of literary mobocracy under which the man in the street has become increasingly the arbiter in matters which he does not understand. To this day only the most modest claims are made for Dickens as an artist and a craftsman, but his position in the affections of the crowd has always been such that criticism has been obliged to accept him and to silence its æsthetic conscience as best it can. This abdication finds its sequel to-day in the endeavor to explain "the significance" of Mr. Sinclair Lewis, and in the general conviction that one person is just as qualified as another to speak as a critic of art and literature. Its apotheosis is found in the attitude defined by Tolstoy in *What is Art?*, where that logician of primitive Christianity carries his concern for the masses to the point at which almost every great achievement in the arts is dismissed as unworthy. An entirely new definition of art is his logical solution of the problem at which so many like to tinker—the problem of how to make art subserve a moralistic end and also remain within the reach of uneducated and undeveloped minds.

CHARLES DICKENS

Better, it seems, that infantilism be the lot of the artist than that the limitations of the mob be exposed by confrontation with matters above its level. Under a Christian democracy Tolstoy's book should be the official primer of æsthetics, for it is the only complete exposition of the ideas with which less honest minds eternally strive to compromise.

It is highly significant that Charles Dickens is one of the few writers of accepted renown who is frequently cited with approval by Tolstoy. He is the predestined glory of the evangelical literary world and the perfect model of the bourgeois Anglo-Saxon genius. He is genial, vulgar, boisterous, sentimental, and full of good intentions. He never looks a problem straight in the face if he can help it, and his flight from reality is so instinctive that he can visualize the worst social conditions, the most repulsive human types, the most tragic circumstances only in terms of the grotesque or the melodramatic. We are constantly reminded of the immortal types which Dickens has given to the whole English-speaking world: Bill Sikes is the burglar incarnate, Mrs. Gamp the nurse, Bumble the beadle, and Squeers the schoolmaster. To mention such personages as Sam Weller, the Artful Dodger, Mr. Micawber, Uriah Heep, Mr. Podsnap, Pecksniff, Mark Tapley, and a host of others, is to conjure up at once as definite a character as a person one knows in actual life. Yet the slightest reflection will show that these creations are as unreal as the heroes and heroines of the Pollyanna school of fiction. Bill Sikes and Nancy are a criminal and his girl, a pair from which those who most delight in Dickens would be the first to shrink had anything of the reality been allowed into Dickens's picture of them. Mr. Micawber is the kind of man whom his friends soon learn to avoid and whose selfish imbecility usually destroys the happiness of those who unfortunately depend upon him.

Not only does Dickens conceal all that these people really are, but his perverse sense of humor leads him to show a marked preference for getting his fun out of what is manifestly horrible or depressing to anyone with a sensitive but realistic imagination. When one begins to recall the scenes and characters which have remained as examples of Dickens's humorous fancies, one finds that an enormous number of them are intrinsically quite the opposite of funny. Dotheboys Hall and Mr. Squeers are assuredly far from laughable; Quilp is a disgusting brute; Mrs. Nickleby a dreadful infliction upon her daughter; the Reverend Mr. Stiggins a repulsive, snivelling creature; the Marchioness a painfully overworked drudge. Yet,

CHARLES DICKENS

so incurable was Dickens's sentimentalism that he could present all this sordidness, brutality, poverty, and crime without ever making their reality felt, while congratulating himself on his "realism." "I will not abate one hole in the Dodger's coat, or one scrap of curl-paper in the girl's dishevelled hair," he writes, and one is reminded of the tears and patches on a stage costume representing poverty.

In what seems to me a strenuous effort to lend some significance to the fact that Dickens survives, while his friend and collaborator Wilkie Collins is dead, like most of his contemporaries, it is said that he was a great instrument of reform, a champion of the poor, an incarnation of the sturdy virtues of Merrie England. If the description of Dotheboys Hall reformed the English school system, then Early Victorian England was more susceptible to gentle reproof than the history of the period indicates. The Chartist movement, the Land war in Ireland, the factory legislation of Lord Shaftesbury, and so forth are not precisely evidence that social changes were so easily effected as this theory of Dickens as the scourge of evil would imply. Neither his Bumble nor his Micawber gives any more sense of the cruelty of the Poor Law and of imprisonment for debt than his Nancy conveys the impression of being an authentic specimen of her class. His world is one of such grotesque unreality that it would be as plausible to argue that Marie Corelli's *Wormwood* aroused France and Switzerland to prohibit absinthe, as to see in *Nicholas Nickleby* or *Oliver Twist* historic documents in the history of social reform in England.

That Dickens himself had some illusion as to the reformist mission of his writings is undeniable, but his intentions need not be accepted for achievements. When the late Miss Marie Corelli wrote such masterpieces as *The Sorrows of Satan* and *Temporal Power* she had as assuredly a serious aim as had her distinguished competitor when he wrote *The Christian*. But in their unreal worlds of melodrama it is impossible to take seriously the situations described, even though one be as horrified as Miss Corelli herself was when she showed us a depraved young English girl reading Swinburne and smoking a cigarette. Propagandist fiction is bad enough in all conscience, but were it added to the other defects in Dickens he would not be read as he is to this day. Fortunately for him, his propaganda was so divorced from reality that none of his readers ever slept a wink the less on that account, just as the equal esteem in which Marie Corelli was held by the plain people was in no wise determined by their indignation at the turpitude which she professed to uncover.

The aim of Dickens was primarily to amuse, and

in this respect he was so obliging that he would alter a story to make it more pleasant. When his Jewish customers protested against Fagin he provided Aaron in *Our Mutual Friend* just to show that there were noble Jews as well as the other kind. His ambition was not to express himself, except in terms of what he held in common with the average reader, but to express the point of view of his public at any cost. In other words, Dickens had all the requisites for the manufacture of digestive fiction, and he is the legitimate ancestor of the innumerable brood that has followed him in that lucrative business. The notion that popular circulationists write with tongue in cheek is erroneous. They always conceive of themselves as having a lofty purpose and, like Dickens, they imagine that they can deal with problems, with the harsher aspects of life, without bringing blushes to supposititious cheeks, and without really getting below the surface. What seems to less commonplace minds a lack of artistic integrity becomes in them that most precious of all illusions, a moral purpose. They claim to be far more effective than their less fortunately constituted colleagues in that the very sweetness and delicacy of their method enable them to build up a huge following and to reach thousands who would not respond to the unpleasant truth.

LITERARY BLASPHEMIES

Dickens was born into English literature just at the moment when the ideals of Victorianism demanded a writer who could triumphantly realize them without doing violence to his own ideals. Whereas a Thackeray had at least the grace to admit that it had become impossible for an English novelist to emulate the author of *Tom Jones,* Dickens professed to have been greatly inspired and influenced by Fielding and Smollett, but made no complaint against the conventions which were emasculating the English novel. He was in his element in a society whose ears were stopped with cotton wool, and where taboos so virulently flourished that the expression "Early Victorianism" was to become the synonym for unhealthy prudery and self-complacent ugliness based on what we now know to have been sheer intellectual dishonesty. The result is that the modern reader can respect only those isolated figures who miraculously escaped the prevailing blight and are rewarded in our esteem for the actual or comparative neglect which was their fate at the hands of the Victorian public. If Charlotte Brontë, or Jane Austen before her, had reflected the popular taste as Dickens did, one might have more respect both for the English novel and for the voice of the people as the voice of literary criticism.

The newly arising middle-class, with the carrot

CHARLES DICKENS

of progress dangling before its nose and the dawn of the industrial era filling the skies with clouds of smoke, very naturally demanded the literature to which it could respond, and the supply was forthcoming. There was the dreary tribe of women novelists of both sexes, the George Eliots, Gaskells, Trollopes, and worse, with Dickens leading them on. Under his reign, as much as under Victoria's, English fiction allowed its feet to be bound in bonds so tight and deforming that the cramped and almost atrophied muscles are only now beginning slowly to recover their old suppleness. The undoubtedly great talent of Dickens did not suffer under the constraints which hampered and delayed greater men who followed him immediately, like Thomas Hardy, George Meredith, and Samuel Butler. He easily accepted the postulates which governed the writing of fiction during the first three-quarters of the nineteenth century in England, postulates which make one marvel all the more because of the wonderful beginnings to which they promised an ignominious end. After Defoe, Fielding, Smollett, and Sterne, these purveyors to the legendary "Young Person" were a feeble succession in a line so mighty that the Continent had learned the craft of fiction from the British novelists. Now came the novel made chemically pure by resolute evasion and timid euphemism, romanticizing the home, sentimentalizing distress, substituting marriage for love, and in its endeavor to eliminate sex almost obliterating what was known at the time as the Sex. To enumerate the omissions and defects of the Victorian novel is to sum up the entire stock in trade of Dickens: his inability to describe women who are not either morons or comic stage characters, his avoidance of passion until its wicked fruits can be dragged in for melodramatic effect, as in the affair of Steerforth and Little Em'ly and the story of Lady Dedlock in *Bleak House,* his young girls who are just pale puppets to be used for the introduction of marriage bells and, in general, his tiresome insistence on foibles and eccentricities in lieu of characterization, his substitution of masks for faces.

It is not for nothing that the era of Dickens saw the decline of the English novel from a first-rate achievement for adult minds to a distraction for children and an aid to digestion. The genius for fiction, frustrated in England, found expression in France where the preoccupations of the literary world were far removed indeed from debates as to whether *Oliver Twist* was not an immortal glorification of crime. Balzac had produced a large part of his colossal work, and *Eugénie Grandet, Père Goriot* and *Les Illusions perdues* made an appearance which coincided with that of *Sketches by*

CHARLES DICKENS

Boz, Pickwick Papers, Oliver Twist, and *Nicholas Nickleby.* When England was wallowing in the bathos of Little Nell, Stendhal published *La Chartreuse de Parme.* Between 1833 and 1853, the years when Dickens's fame and popularity reached their highest point, Balzac was pouring out of his wonderful fecundity the finest volumes of his Human Comedy; and he was then a man with a vast quantity of work behind him, sufficient in quantity to have at least begun to exhaust the imaginative vigor of a lesser writer. In the prodigious canon of his writings—which the bibliographers list in more than three hundred titles—there is much rubbish; even in the more modest compass in which his collected works are preserved, many volumes could be spared. All that is conceded as to Balzac's lack of style makes his case somewhat analogous to that of Dickens, whose defects are frankly admitted by most critics. Yet there can be no comparison of these two novelists who dominated the fiction of their country in the early nineteenth century. Balzac was a great creative genius who made the modern French novel. Dickens was an energetic entertainer whose success helped materially to unmake the modern English novel.

During the twenty-year period mentioned Dickens published *Sketches by Boz, The Pickwick*

LITERARY BLASPHEMIES

Papers, Oliver Twist, Nicholas Nickleby, The Old Curiosity Shop, Dombey and Son, David Copperfield, and *Bleak House,* which are not only the books of his own heyday but also those upon which his posthumous popularity chiefly rests; they are the quintessence of all that is Dickensian. They all belong to that first half of the nineteenth century whose ingenuous self-satisfaction with the shibboleths bequeathed by the then deceased and therefore respected French Revolution is so well reflected in Macauley's *History of England.* Smug piety and domesticity enjoyed the highest sanction and example of the Court, and the country had the popular literature it deserved. But the turn of the century was to witness the first uneasy stirrings of a conviction that all was not well, and by 1859, when Darwin published *The Origin of Species,* the political and theological illusions necessary to the existence of Victorianism were being rudely shaken. Even Dickens was touched to some extent by the movement of ideas, and during the last fifteen years of his life his writings showed traces of a less unscrupulous optimism. In 1854 *Hard Times* appeared, followed by *Little Dorrit, A Tale of Two Cities, Great Expectations, Our Mutual Friend* and the unfinished *Edwin Drood.* These are the works which are credited with a real seriousness, and in them, if anywhere,

CHARLES DICKENS

the claim of Dickens to be regarded as more than a puppet master must be found.

"One or two passages of exquisite pathos and the rest sullen Socialism" was an eminently Victorian contemporary's judgment on *Hard Times*. In reality, the book is the nearest approach Dickens made to realism, in the sense that he places his scenes not in some phantasmagoric world of his imagination but in the Potteries, and his characters are recognizable types rather than caricatures. Coketown is presented, not as a slum with picturesque possibilities, but as an ordinary factory town such as Arnold Bennett might describe. Its smoke and dirt, its miserable population, its masters Gradgrind and Bounderby are no longer subjects for humorous embroidery. Dickens is content to describe them as they are and to use them to point the moral of his great discovery: that the industrial revolution meant not progress but the degradation of civilization. Mrs. Gamp and Quilp and Bill Sikes are not precisely charming people, but in their presentation by Dickens many people profess to be charmed by them. Nobody has found Gradgrind and Bounderby charming, although through sheer force of habit Dickens tries halfheartedly to make comic figures of them by his usual device of emphasizing oddities of speech and demeanor. Having described Bounderby drumming on his hat as if it were a tambourine, Dickens proceeds to add, "Mr. Bounderby put his tambourine on his head, like an oriental dancer." He provides Sleary with a stage lisp worthy of a burlesque show and, having created a relatively credible young woman in Louisa Gradgrind, he puts her through melodramatic paces comparable to those of Edith Dombey. If there is anything worse in Dickens than the scene in which Louisa tells her father that she nearly succumbed to Harthouse, either in its stilted language or its general unconvincingness, I have not discovered it.

In *Hard Times* Dickens has largely resisted that perverse desire of his to make all loathsome creatures funny, but he still clings to the corollary of that method: he makes tragic figures theatrical and flies ignominiously from all manifestations of the elementary human passions. He either cannot—as I think—or will not create character and analyze human motives and impulses. We must be grateful when, as in *Hard Times,* he succeeds in showing us types undistorted by his resolve to be whimsical under all circumstances. Ordinarily types are abstractions which we do not accept for living human beings in the works of greater novelists. But Dickens felt so strongly the theme of *Hard Times* that he—perhaps unwittingly—planted certain types squarely before us. Better than the hackneyed passage about Gradgrind the man of facts, is this sketch of the self-made ignoramus:

Vagabond, errand-boy, labourer, porter, clerk, chief manager, small partner, Josiah Bounderby of Coketown. Those are the antecedents, and the culmination. Josiah Bounderby of Coketown learnt his letters from the outsides of the shops, Mrs. Gradgrind, and was first able to tell the time upon a dial-plate, from studying the steeple clock at St. Giles's Church, London, under the direction of a drunken cripple, who was a convicted thief and an incorrigible vagrant. Tell Josiah Bounderby of Coketown, of your district schools and your model schools, and your training schools, and your whole kettle-of-fish of schools; and Josiah Bounderby of Coketown tells you plainly, all right, all correct—he hadn't such advantages—but let us have hard-headed, solid-fisted people—the education that made him won't do for everybody, he knows well—such and such his education was, however, and you may force him to swallow boiling fat, but you shall never force him to suppress the facts of his life.

Unlike some of the other horrors which Dickens described, this one, so far as I know, is not counted among those with whose abolition he is credited. Even the formula for describing this Early Victorian Babbitt is still working well. Another phenomenon of modern times is also well recorded in this epic of industrial progress:

LITERARY BLASPHEMIES

There was a native organization in Coketown itself, whose members were to be heard of in the House of Commons every session, indignantly petitioning for acts of parliament that should make these people religious by main force. Then came the Teetotal Society, who complained that these same people *would* get drunk, and showed in tabular statements that they did get drunk, and proved at tea parties that no inducement, human or Divine (except a medal), would induce them to forego their custom of getting drunk. Then came the chemist and the druggist, with other tabular statements, showing that when they didn't get drunk, they took opium. Then came the experienced chaplain of the jail, with more tabular statements, outdoing all the previous tabular statements, and showing that the same people *would* resort to low haunts, hidden from the public eye, where they heard low singing and saw low dancing, and mayhap joined in it; and where A. B., aged twenty-four next birthday, and committed for eighteen months' solitary, had himself said (not that he had ever shown himself particularly worthy of belief) his ruin began, as he was perfectly sure and confident that otherwise he would have been a tip-top moral specimen.

Here, too, is an abuse which Dickens somehow failed to abolish, no doubt because, as these two quotations indicate, *Hard Times* lacks that genial note which turned Nancy into a sweet young thing and made Quilp just a quaint little creature. It is the harshest of all his works and one of the least popular. It is, to quote Bernard Shaw, "the first fruit of that very interesting occurrence which our religious sects call, sometimes conversion, sometimes attaining to conviction of sin . . . the occasional indignation has spread and deepened into a passionate revolt against the whole industrial order of the modern world. Here you will find no more villains and heroes, but only oppressors and victims, oppressing and suffering in spite of themselves, driven by a huge machinery which grinds to pieces the people it should nourish and ennoble, and having for its directors the basest and the most foolish instead of the noblest and most farsighted."

Mr. Shaw is, of course, trying to persuade himself that, having touched earth for once, Dickens is to be hailed at this point as a Socialist, probably the only occasion when Bernard Shaw and Lord Macaulay ever found themselves in agreement. "Entirely right in main drift and purpose" was Ruskin's comment, which leaves the novel as such uncriticized. Looking at the book to-day, one is more impressed by its crudities than by its virtues when compared with the works of the earlier manner. Mr. Sleary, Cissy Jupe, Rachel and Stephen Blackpool are honest, noble, God-fearing, unselfish workers contrasted mechanically with the hardness and swinishness of the Gradgrinds and Bounderbys. Slackbridge, the trade-union organizer, is a middleclass bogey, as incredible, as unrelated to the truth as Dickens's equally bourgeois misconceptions about the aristocracy. He sees the trade unions with the same eyes as Gradgrind, and describes the meetings of Slackbridge with all the ignorance of a man who hated to remember that he once worked in a blacking factory. If Dickens had possessed that insight into the minds and hearts of the working classes with which his radical as well as his sentimental admirers endow him, it is strange that this "apostle of the people," as Edwin Pugh calls him, could be guilty of the middleclass snobbery of *Hard Times*. The truth is that this book simply stands outside the previous limits which Dickens had set himself; it does not stand higher, because at best it has the qualities of Charles Kingsley: it is mid-Victorian radicalism.

Little Dorrit, his next book, is another attempt on the part of Dickens to write seriously. The difference between it and his previous work is more obviously illustrated by the fact that it treats realistically a theme which the author had already treated fantastically. Edward Dorrit's disintegration under pressure of financial circumstances is the true story with which Dickens trifled when he drew his picture of Mr. Micawber. It is, I think, significant and typical of the problem with which Dickens confronts the modern reader that Edward

CHARLES DICKENS

Dorrit is probably the obscurest character in the Dickens repertory whereas Micawber is one of the most familiar. Dorrit is one of the rare instances of honest analysis in the writings of Dickens, Micawber is one of the many instances of sentimental embellishment; the former is forgotten, the latter is remembered. What is even more significant of the attitude of those who admire Dickens is the bewildered speculation as to how the same person, to wit, the novelist's father, could serve as the model for both Micawber and Dorrit—a bewilderment as naïve as that which might be produced by comparing the antics of a drunken man as seen by a boon companion with those antics as reported by the policeman who arrested them. The moment that Dickens describes anything as it exists in reality, we are warned that he is not himself. By one of those sardonic strokes of fate which were peculiarly numerous, as we have subsequently discovered, in the unspacious times of Queen Victoria, the life of Dickens refused to become a part of his scheme of things. The coryphant of domesticity could not live with his own wife. The anxieties of that crisis are urged in extenuation of the fact that it was then that he wrote *Little Dorrit*, a story with an unhappy ending.

We are entitled to congratulate ourselves that he did not live in this so enlightened and uninhibited age, when he would assuredly have found it both necessary and desirable to transform his domestic affairs into copy. Let us be content to note that when the bottom dropped out of Dickens's universe he also dropped his rose-colored spectacles and attempted to see life steadily, if not whole. The consequence was that in *Little Dorrit* he has left some satire which it is still possible to read with enjoyment, the picture of the Circumlocution Office, for example, in which the eternal beauties of bureaucracy are enshrined. The essence of parliamentary government is contained in such passages as this:

Then would the noble lord or right honourable gentleman, in whose department it was to defend the Circumlocution Office, put an orange in his pocket, and make a regular field-day of the occasion. Then would he come down to that house with a slap upon the table and meet the honourable gentleman foot to foot. Then would he be there to tell that honourable gentleman that the Circumlocution Office was not only blameless in this matter, but was commendable in this matter, was extollable to the skies in this matter. Then would he be there to tell that honourable gentleman that although the Circumlocution Office was invariably right, and wholly right, it never was so right as in this matter. Then would he be there to tell the honourable gentleman that it would have been more to his honour, more to his credit, more to his good taste, more to his good sense, more to half the dictionary of common places if he had left the Circumlocution Office alone and never approached this matter. Then would he keep one eye upon a coach or crammer from the Circumlocution Office below the bar, and smash the honourable gentleman with the Circumlocution Office account of this matter. And although one of two things always happened; namely, either that the Circumlocution Office had nothing to say, and said it, or that it had something to say of which the right honourable gentleman blundered one half and forgot the other; the Circumlocution Office was always voted immaculate by an accommodating majority.

The light-hearted Dickens reappears in *Our Mutual Friend,* but in the main his later works are marked by an air of gravity which corresponded to a change in the temper of the times and in the circumstances of the author's own life. It would be an exaggeration to pretend that Dickens, even at this stage, showed any signs of being a man of ideas. In *Hard Times* and *Little Dorrit* there are flashes of genuine satire which enable one to reread those books with less impatience than the more typical works arouse, but the essential childishness and superficiality of Dickens are inescapable. Balzac had died before Dickens entered this final phase of his career, but already another Frenchman had arisen to dwarf him. *Little Dorrit* was published the same year as *Madame Bovary,* and the mere juxtaposition of the two at once settles the place of the English novelist; he is simply not grown up. Furthermore, both Dickens and Flaubert established a line of fiction, and the one is infantile while the other is adult. To a superlative degree Dickens embodied that quality of mawkish respectability which differentiates modern English fiction from that of Continental Europe.

When Washington Irving wrote to Dickens of "that exquisite tact that enabled him to carry his reader through the veriest dens of vice and villainy without a breath to shock the ear or a stain to sully the robe of the most shrinking delicacy" he undoubtedly expressed an appreciation which is widely shared. In fact the same testimony has been proudly paid to a vast school of British and American novelists. Yet, may one not legitimately ask what sort of morbid delight is this which brings writer and reader into contact with persons and situations from which they really shrink in horror? If an author likes to linger in "the veriest dens of vice," then intellectual honesty and artistic courage demand that he shall not pretend to be elsewhere. If such scenes have any genuine importance in the execution of his aim it must be because of their intrinsic effectiveness. Otherwise they are mere stage settings, artificial and unconvincing outside the world of pure makebelieve. In fairy tales one does not consider the authenticity of material detail, but we expect of the modern novel something more than a fable for children; and it is because so many of our novelists do not realize this that fiction in English has ceased to offer anything to the intelligence, becoming nothing more than a means amongst others of killing time.

To demand that a writer shall give us only what he is prepared truthfully and honestly to describe is not, as some think, to insist that he shall surpass Zola in the inventorying of Nana's bedroom or Coupeau's kitchen. All that one asks is that, if he introduces us to Nana, she shall not be palmed off as a species of Little Nell. William Dean Howells, according to his latest biographer, wrote forty volumes in which "adultery is never pictured; seduction never; divorce once and sparingly . . . marriage discordant to the point of cleavage, only once and in the same novel with the divorce; crime only once with any fullness; . . . politics never; religion passingly and superficially; science only in crepuscular psychology; mechanics, athletics, bodily exploits or collisions, very rarely." Whatever may be thought of this conception of the function of the novel, Howells had at least the courage of his omissions and did not try to include surreptitiously, as it were, what he conceived to be unpleasant or undesirable. He did not qualify for that strange test of merit which Washington Irving applied to Dickens. It is curious to notice that this list of Howells's taboos is almost a summary of Dickens's themes yet the English novelist was no less squeamish than the American; he was simply less logical.

He was, however, more astute, not deliberately but unwittingly and instinctively; for he was able to satisfy that profound Anglo-Saxon yearning for appearances and compromises. Had Flaubert described Bill Sykes and Nancy, Dickens would not have made it one of his bravura pieces on the lecture platform—nor would Flaubert, for that matter, had he bethought himself of that lucrative aid to literary fame. Nobody ever congratulated the creator of Madame Bovary on having concluded that superb analysis "without a breath to shock the ear," for he so decidedly shocked the ears of the Second Empire that its well-known pruderies were outraged to the point of indicting him. Neither then nor since, nevertheless, could any intelligent person be found to argue that "the robe of the most shrinking delicacy" was stained by Flaubert's regard for his own artistic integrity. Therein lies all the difference between a novelist who knows what the public wants and one who knows only what he himself must and can do, between a great creative genius and a public entertainer. Their aims and their methods are as far apart as their fields; the one deals with life, the other with conventions.

The inevitable conclusion to the premise of the Victorian novel is a literature for grown-up children, which becomes, in the last analysis, a literature to be read in childhood. Hence the statement of Brandes about Scott which I have already quoted, and which may well stand for all that group of read but unreadable nineteenth century English novelists. If one begins young enough to be still in the omnivorous stage of reading it is possible to absorb Dickens with appropriate rapture, and it is sometimes possible to take him up again and see him through the merciful glamour of one's youth. But the spectacle of a person of mature taste encountering Dickens for the first time would have about it an air of incongruity as unbecoming as the sight of a man of forty stuffing himself with cream puffs in schoolboy fashion. The meal would prove also equally indigestible. Such defiances of nature are compatible only with youth. Then the receptive faculties are more developed than the critical, and pleasure is unrestrained by reflection. Thus it is without difficulty that one accepts the conventions of Dickens's unreal world where all the stage properties, scenery, and costumes are of the best quality, but the pretense of life is unsustained. Here are good humor and fantastic imagination, tears and thrills, a delightful fairyland in a realistic setting—everything that makes Charles Dickens an excellent writer for children.

Chapter Seven

EDGAR ALLAN POE

THE high status of Edgar Allan Poe to-day seems to be largely another manifestation of that modern American delight in sin whereby the intelligentsia demonstrate their emancipation from the simple code of their rude forefathers. He is invested with the same glamour of sympathetic wickedness to which may be traced the benevolent smiles that greet all violations of the Eighteenth Amendment in cultivated and enlightened society. Had Poe died in 1925, none but the Anti-Saloon League would have been too poor to do him reverence.

Assuredly, four generations would not have been provoked into trying to prove that he was an honest and noble fellow, devoted to his home life, who obeyed God's commandments, and had no vices worth mentioning—all of which showed that he was a great American writer. Were a Rev. Rufus Wilmot Griswold to arise now and declare his weaknesses, Poe's reputation would be made at once, instead of being postponed until friends began to whitewash him. On the other hand, if those friends and champions—Mrs. Whitman, Eugene L. Didier, William F. Gill, J. H. Ingram, and the rest—had described the real Poe, all interest in him would long since have subsided. The author of "The Raven" and "Annabel Lee" would have a page or two in the anthologies, and the creator of Dupin would be mentioned as the father of the modern detective story, but Poe without Griswold would be half forgotten as an American Tieck or an E. T. A. Hoffmann, a minor contributor to the neglected literature of Gothic romance. In the Poe universe Voltaire's phrase must be adapted. If there were no Griswold, it would be necessary to invent one.

Since the year after Poe's death, when Griswold published his much denounced but now little read Memoir, in the 1850 edition of *The Literati,* a considerable literature has accumulated in defense of Edgar Allan Poe. Although several of his friends, such as G. R. Graham and J. Neal, immediately controverted Griswold, and although N. P. Willis's and J. R. Lowell's very friendly accounts were included by Griswold in his edition of the works of Poe, it is always said that the former poisoned the public mind because his side of the story monopolized the field. Yet, between 1850 and 1880 J. Hannay and J. H. Ingram in England

and L. A. Wilmer, Mrs. Helen Whitman, W. F. Gill, Eugene L. Didier and Mayne Reid in America, prominently challenged what they held to be untrue and unfavorable statements of Griswold. Had his only service been to stimulate the controversies which these writers launched and which still endure, Rufus Wilmot Griswold would be an important factor in keeping Poe's fame alive.

His services as a biographer and literary executor are, however, of a more positive nature. Only a generation determined to kill Poe by kindness could have been so sensitive to Griswold's criticism, which was not only in harmony with the spirit of the times, but tends to create precisely the impression of Poe which guarantees his favorable reception to-day. Most of the indignant successors of Griswold insist that he foully libeled the dead, that he carried calumny and defamatory innuendo to an extreme, and that he acquired Poe's papers and secured the task of editing them by dubious methods, in order to destroy his good name in the eyes of posterity. Yet one of the immediate results of his work as editor was that "the sale reached about fifteen hundred sets every year." It was difficult to find a publisher for the books; "Dr. Griswold," according to a first-hand witness, "had offered the works to nearly all the leading publishers, who declined to undertake the publication." His persistence and final success were surely strange in a man allegedly bent upon ruining Poe.

What a critic who really admired Poe might have said of him, his friends have proved. Here are some phrases from an obituary: "In him literary art lost one of its most brilliant but erratic stars. He printed, in 1827, a small volume of poems, most of which were written in early youth. Some of these poems are quoted in a review by Margaret Fuller, in the *Tribune* in 1846, and are justly regarded as among the most wonderful exhibitions of the precocious development of genius. They illustrated the character of his abilities, and justified his anticipations of success. For a considerable time, however, though he wrote readily and brilliantly, his contributions to the journals attracted little attention, and his hopes of gaining a livelihood by the profession of literature were nearly ended at length in sickness, poverty, and despair." The note of appreciative sympathy is obvious in this reference to his editorship of *The Southern Literary Messenger,* "in which he wrote many brilliant articles and raised the *Messenger* to the first rank of literary periodicals." His talents as a critic, too, are admitted, "in criticism . . . his papers attracted much attention by their careful and skillful analysis and general caus-

EDGAR ALLAN POE

tic severity," while *Tales of the Grotesque and Arabesque* "established his reputation for ingenuity, imagination, and extraordinary power in tragical narration."

His powers as a writer are not allowed to obscure his other qualities. "His conversation was at times almost supramortal in its eloquence. His voice was modulated with astonishing skill, and his large and variably expressive eyes looked repose or shot fiery tumult into theirs who listened. . . . His imagery was from the worlds which no mortal can see, but with the vision of genius . . . he rejected the forms of customary logic, and in a crystalline process of accretion, built up his ocular demonstrations in forms of gloomiest and ghostliest grandeur, or in those of the most airy and delicious beauty." To sum up: "As a writer of tales it will be admitted generally that he was scarcely surpassed in ingenuity of construction or effective painting; as a critic, he was more remarkable as a dissector of sentences than as a commenter upon ideas. He was little better than a carping grammarian. As a poet he will retain a most honorable rank. . . . In poetry, as in prose, he was most successful in the metaphysical treatment of the passions. His poems are constructed with wonderful ingenuity, and finished with consummate art. They illustrate a morbid sensitiveness of feeling, a shadowy and gloomy imagination, and a taste almost faultless in the apprehension of that sort of beauty most agreeable to his temper."

These quotations from an article hastily written on receipt of the news of his death contain only one reservation as to Poe's abilities as a writer. He was not a critic who could expound ideas, but was more concerned with syntax and those fine points in the use of English which can rarely be raised without provoking the charge of grammatical pedantry from a people notoriously impatient with purists. This typical response of the English-speaking reader to his grammarians is the one venial sin in a series of critical comments which do not aim at an inclusive profundity, but do correspond, in the main, to what succeeding generations have said about Edgar Allan Poe. They are all quoted, from the obituary of Poe written by the legendary arch-fiend, Rufus Wilmot Griswold, "that villain," as he came to be known to the doting lady friends of the deceased, and their literary *cavaliers servants.*

As that article at once drew upon its author the wrath of Poe's friends, it is hardly surprising that the Memoir excited even greater indignation. Griswold would not have been human, much less a very typical "literary gent," if he had not tried to defend himself against the accusations which his obituary had provoked. He had either to write himself down a knave or prove his charges against Poe, and to that end he prepared his Memoir, delaying its appearance until two volumes of the Collected Works had appeared. The delay is mentioned as an example of his diabolical cunning, whereas it must be apparent that the circumstances demanded time for the preparation of a detailed defense of the attitude which Griswold had taken in sharply distinguishing between Poe the man and Poe the writer. Had he wished merely to injure, he would not have allowed the volumes containing the work most likely to attract popular attention to appear under the entirely benevolent ægis of N. P. Willis and J. R. Lowell.

The Memoir, naturally, is chiefly concerned with the personality rather than the work of Poe. What are the revelations contained in it which have earned for Griswold an immortal infamy? Nothing more nor less than that Poe was irascible, inconsistent, cynical, impecunious, unreliable, and frequently drunk. Some of the instances cited of his behavior when under the influence of one or all of these phases of his character have been denied by persons no more disinterested in their friendship than Griswold in his hostility. Certain incidents, we may take it, are inaccurately reported, but it is difficult to see any important respect in which the Memoir is untrue. When we are told that Poe's parting from Mrs. Whitman was accompanied by a drunken scene in which the police had to intervene, the lady herself repudiates the suggestion. But her own story proves that Poe's drunkenness was the obstacle to their marriage, and we must console ourselves with the thought that his conduct was "eccentric," "distraught," or whatever charitable adjective seems to be most appropriate.

It is in their selection of charitable euphemisms and the ingenious pleading of extenuating circumstances that the apologists of Poe differentiate themselves from those who are accused, like Griswold, of being malevolent; or like Professor Woodberry, of being too coldly judicial. The facts are often garbled, and the substitution of "correct" versions has diverted the leisure of many commentators since Ingram led the way. The contempt of these champions of Poe for one another and their reciprocal charges of distortion and dishonesty are perhaps the best comment upon the futility of the Griswold legend. His misdeeds, real and imaginary, are the only ground upon which they all agree. For the rest, Gill despises Ingram as a prevaricator; Ingram ignores Gill's *Life of Poe,* although it forestalled many points in his own, and both fall upon Eugene L. Didier in a manner unsurpassed by Griswold at his worst. Even Mrs. Whitman, who had obvious reasons for supporting the work of rehabilitation, is not treated as being above suspicion. Having refused to marry Poe, she was united to him in bonds more enduring, for she supplied most of the facts and a great deal of the whitewash to the anti-Griswold biographers. Their tasks were, however, complicated by the fact that she was not the only extant old lady who had memories of the time when she was, thought she was, or had hopes of being, the only woman who really understood the poet and was designed to be his affinity.

Poe's penchant for women older than himself was manifested while he was still a schoolboy, when he fell in love with Mrs. Jane Stith Stanard. It was Mrs. Clemm, not Virginia, the consumptive child, who was the real companion of his home life, and to the end, as the final encounters with Mrs. Whitman and Mrs. Shelton show, he was attracted by that type of maturity. While besieging the romantic Mrs. Whitman in appropriate terms of exaltation, he was simultaneously appealing to the motherly or sisterly instincts of Mrs. Annie Richmond, to whom he wrote: "Of one thing rest assured, from this day forth I shun the pestilential society of *literary women*. They are a heartless, unnatural, venomous and dishonorable set, with no guiding principle but inordinate self-esteem. Mrs. Osgood is the only exception I know." When the zealous Ingram revealed this correspondence with "Annie," Mrs. Whitman was somewhat disturbed; but this time Griswold could not be blamed, nor proven a liar by reference to the obvious facts of Poe's indebtedness to some of these ladies. He did not repay them all, as he repaid Mrs. Lewis, by puffing her bad verses and inducing others to do so by promising to return the favor. After his death, as Mrs. Whitman's letters reveal, Mrs. Clemm carried on the family tradition of exploiting the sentimental weakness of her sex for "Eddie."

His female admirers, in the last analysis, were a greater asset than he perhaps could have foreseen. "Poe's Helen" was the author of the first book in his defense, when *Edgar Poe and his Critics,* by Sarah Helen Whitman, appeared in 1860. This work gave the cue to all her successors, and most of them actually got from her and her rivals, authentic or spurious, the data to which their fond but unreliable memories lent an air of verisimilitude. The process of whitewashing Poe became at once an effort to reconcile the brutal frankness of his harsh critics and the ingenuous apologies of less candid men friends with the haloed figure that haunted the closing years of his "feminine coterie," to quote Miss Ticknor. "Lovely woman," she adds, "who in her youth inspires immortal verse, may prove in later years to be unwieldy, unattractive, and commonplace, as well as an unscrupulous busybody, quite ready to exploit herself at the expense of one whose brief attention has alone rescued her from oblivion." Nevertheless, but for Griswold and the coterie so composed, American literature would lack its one dramatic and controversial chapter.

Poe very naturally did not display himself in his worst moments to the literary ladies, although most of them had had personal proof of his unfortunate "affliction." Like all men who want to be mothered, he had a highly romantic conception of what a "good woman" should be, and it is not surprising that the testimony of his women friends rarely coincides with that of the men, and when it does, the same incident is bathed in a softened light. Griswold and Lowell saw Poe when he was drunk and his restraints were cast off. In the drawing-room of Waverly Place the admiring poetesses saw the lion of the hour, the author of "The Raven," the American Werther, an irresistibly sad, romantic, *beau ténébreux*. Of course they thought it was horrid of Dr. Griswold to talk of hiccoughs, of articles altered for friendship's or money's sake, of the squabbles and shifts and compromises in the ups and downs of an impecunious literary gentleman's life. They had gazed into those beautiful eyes, and had heard that voice whose eloquence thrilled even Griswold. When he wrote about the female literati, few felt the sting of his pen, which rarely forgot the gallantry due to what was still called the weaker sex.

It is unnecessary to confront Griswold's Poe with the Poe described by thwarted or satisfied romance. Poe's own revelation of himself clears the atmosphere of much cant. In the letters between Allan and Poe, which have at last been published, the picture of the man whom Griswold knew is first sketched. Here is the proud, quarrelsome, penniless author, who has neither the cunning to adapt himself to his environment or to emancipate himself from it. His attitude towards his adoptive father is very similar to his subsequent attitude towards the writers and the literature of his time. He alternately defies and submits, wheedles and threatens, but depends, none the less, upon help which he spurns, demands, and, in the long run, receives. Allan's indifference to the extremely pathetic appeals of his adopted son strikes one at first, on reading the correspondence, but examination shows how frequently money was actually sent and help extended. Allan assuredly was not impressed by Poe the writer, and in retrospect this blindness may seem unpardonable. But with Poe, the helpless human being, despite atrocious quarrels, his conduct was patient, all things considered.

In embryo the Poe-Allan letters contain the whole story of his career. They are original documents which have not been manipulated by any malevolent editor, and they justify Griswold's general conception of the man Poe. Weak and inconsistent, Poe could insult Allan and then accept his charity, as he attacked Griswold and then tried to conciliate him. He made melodramatic demonstrations of independence which he could not carry through, as he displayed a pretended freedom from critical compromises which were common to his colleagues and himself, as they well knew. It ill became him to sneer at Griswold for being too accommodating in his praise, when Poe himself stretched a point in favor of his friends and even induced Griswold and others to abet him in doing so. Allan, already suspect of the crime of *lèse-Poe*, became increasingly involved in the ignominy heaped on all who saw the poet as he really was. Yet, with the letters of Poe to Allan before us, the fundamental soundness of Griswold's estimate of Poe's character would seem to be beyond dispute.

The writer, as distinct from the man, suffered

LITERARY BLASPHEMIES

little from the adverse judgments with which the bulk of Poe literature has been concerned. Ironically, this "rehabilitation" largely takes the form of a denial of those very elements in Poe's life and work which attracted to him Baudelaire, who is unanimously credited with having laid the foundations of Poe's world fame. Baudelaire, however, was by no means the pioneer of Poe in France, as the real facts, which all the biographers have reported incorrectly, will show.

The first record of Poe in French is in the *Revue Britannique* for November, 1845, where "The Gold Bug" was translated by A. Borghers. In 1853 the same translator issued a volume of selected tales which was Poe's first French appearance in book form. There was an anonymous version of "The Murders in the Rue Morgue" in the *Quotidienne* in June, 1846, and in October the same story appeared in the *Commerce,* translated by E. D. Forgues, who had meanwhile given "A Descent into the Maelstrom" to the *Revue Britannique,* and who published the first French study of Poe in the *Revue des Deux Mondes* of October 15, 1846. Baudelaire's first translation, *Mesmeric Revelation,* did not appear until 1848, and it was preceded by several translations, made in 1847 by an American lady, Mme. Isabelle Meunier. In spite of a lawsuit and a great deal of publicity provoked by Forgues, French criticism did not at once succumb to Poe. Baudelaire's translations achieved the results with which he is credited, but even he could not induce Sainte-Beuve to give his support, which would seem to indicate that New England self-sufficiency and personal spite were not the only factors militating against Poe's success. Sainte-Beuve was neither a "Frogpondian" nor a Griswold.

The literary affinity of Baudelaire and Poe played an admittedly great part in the latter's rise to fame. In France the disciples of Poe through Baudelaire have been frequently enumerated— Villiers de l'Isle Adam, Verlaine, Rimbaud, and Mallarmé; the whole Symbolist Movement has been traced back to him through this lineage. The latest poet of that tradition to be admitted to the French Academy, Paul Valéry, has been characterized in the presence of the five Academies, united in solemn session, as the living exponent, with Poe, Baudelaire, and Mallarmé of "pure poetry"—not in the sense of George Moore's anthology, but meaning poetry which relies upon sound and mood rather than ideas for its effects. The Academician who propounded this idea, however, insisted that Poe had been anticipated about the middle of the eighteenth century by the Reverend Père Rapin, perpetual secretary of the French Academy, so that the honors of the platitude do not strictly belong to Poe.

French criticism, in its enthusiasm, has gone even further, for Poe's title to have invented the modern detective story has been modified by the literary genealogists. The newspaper serial came into being in France about the middle of the nineteenth century, and the kind of public for which the *feuilleton* catered demanded the sensationalism of decaying Romanticism. It was this vogue which gave Poe his first hearing in France, and the first adaptation of the "Murders in the Rue Morgue" was used as a stop-gap until the next serial was ready. Poe's Dupin is Vidocq improved by the application of Laplace's theory of mathematical analysis, according to a French critic, who points out that Poe knew the *Memoirs* of Vidocq, and tried in *Eureka* to carry further the method of Laplace. Voltaire, however, was his true ancestor, for Dupin possesses "the ingenuity of Zadig, the astuteness of Vidocq, and even something of Laplace's mathematical genius." Poe, however, has one claim to complete originality. He created the honest detective, no longer an ex-convict, but a learned man, who regards crime as a scientific problem and is sympathetic to the reader. If Poe's work still lives, it is because of that quality which made his stories suitable material for the French *feuilleton.* He is read as the author of *Tales of Mystery and Imagination,* and not as the mystic poet or the profound philosopher whom ingenious commentators have imagined. His most recent French biographer, Camille Mauclair, has carried the process of exaggeration so far as to establish a parallel between Poe and Leonardo da Vinci, seeing in both a fusion of poetry and mathematics, and arguing that even his tales were to Poe primarily exercises in form, their content of mystery or horror being of minor importance and quite beneath the notice of the author of *Eureka.* As to that chaos of vague ideas, neither he nor any of his predecessors can give any convincing account of it. Poe is a great thinker, it seems, but the work which he himself regarded as the supreme expression of his philosophy remains unintelligible even to those who wish to be convinced of its wisdom.

If Poe's critical writings have shown a tendency to rise in modern esteem, it must be by way of compensation for the neglect of his other works. While the legend persisted, with its perpetual flux of controversy, some justification in the writings themselves had to be found for the disproportionate interest in Poe. As the bulk of his poetry fully justifies Emerson's reference to "the jingle man," and his narrative prose bears all the marks of the excruciating, florid tastelessness of the period, consolation was sought in his criticism. Superficially this part of his work presents certain characteristics which seem to bring him closer to the temper of present-day American literature. He protested against provincial subservience to England in literary matters, and he never failed to remind the "Frogpondians" that New England was not America, that Boston was not the only place where American literature was being produced.

In this argument the wish was evidently father to the literature, for, even when he is accusing Lowell of ignoring Southerners, he cites only such names as Legaré, Simms, and Longstreet as examples of Southern authors of note. The list of names in *The Literati* consists of the illustrious unknown, the "Grub-Street and Dunciad populace," as George Woodberry called it, "with the disadvantages of a large female immigration into these purlieus." It is only necessary to recall the elementary facts of the literary history of America to see that, even with Irving, Cooper, and Bryant thrown in for good measure, literature outside New England was as unimportant as it appeared in the perspective of Boston. Poe's obscure members of the Knickerbocker school add nothing to the claims he implied, rather than asserted. It has been said that these essays on his New York contemporaries were not deliberately chosen by Poe, but were the result of his activities as a reviewer of current literature. If, however, such chapters be withdrawn from his critical writings, what remains to support the theory that he was a fine critic? He wrote of his friends and contemporaries in New York just as Lowell wrote of *his* friends and contemporaries in Boston. Poe mistook geographical accident for critical detachment. He was as blind to the defects of most of the literati as the most self-complacent Bostonian to the minor New Englanders.

There remain a handful of essays of a general critical nature and his estimates of foreign writers to substantiate the belief that Poe was a critic of unusual powers. His analysis of *Barnaby Rudge* and his anticipation of the development of the plot are still mentioned as great achievements, but, as the Dickensians have not failed to point out, Poe was wrong in all his deductions. His final essay on the subject is an attempt to prove Dickens guilty of defective technique because his story did not develop as Poe predicted it would. *Rienzi* is reviewed as "a profound and lucid exposition of the *morale* of Government," in addition to being "a glorious, a wonderful conception" as a fiction. Lever, on the other hand, is denounced as a vulgarian, and Macaulay's syntax is corrected. Elizabeth Barrett Browning shares the author's approval with Elizabeth Oakes Smith, Amelia Welby, Estelle Anna Lewis, and Frances Sargent Osgood, amongst others of her sex.

"The Philosophy of Composition" and "The Poetic Principle" are the two most elaborate expositions of Poe's fundamental ideas of literary criticism. In the former he attempts an explanation of the genesis of "The Raven" at which even Baudelaire revolted, and the general consensus of opinion ever since has been that no poet ever composed in the mechanical and mathematical manner suggested. It is, however, probable that an element of truth underlay the theory, which was built up, as his stories were constructed, by beginning at the end. This would explain much of the obvious, meretricious quality of such poems as are typically Poesque. "The Poetic Principle" is another *a posteriori* account of the author's own conception of poetry, with its premise that a long poem is a contradiction in terms, leading up to the discovery that didacticism is the negation of art, but truth is beauty, and poetry is "the Rhythmical Creation of Beauty."

Like so much theory of criticism, these principles of Poe's have little practical interest, for he resembles all critical theorists in that his practice, when confronted with a work of art, was very much like that of critics unencumbered by theories. Whatever is theoretically sound and practicable is simply a platitude; the rest is intellectual gymnastics. Criticism stands or falls not by its theories, but by the achievements of the critic endowed with taste and experience. If he is corrupt, ignorant, or stupid, the soundness of his philosophical principles is of slight concern. Compared with Lowell, Poe does not show himself superior in his ability to estimate contemporary values. He had a sharp pen and, when it was feasible, he would display harsh humor and contemptuous independence in his judgments. But he did not always find it feasible, so that his dissection of William Ellery Channing has not the force of Macaulay's execution of Montgomery because Macaulay has left no laudation of an Estelle Anna Lewis to mitigate our admiration for his discerning courage. With critics of real quality, Hazlitt and Coleridge and Sainte-Beuve, it would simply be unreasonable to compare their American contemporary. Poe was, indeed, "a dissector of sentences," talking "like a book of iambs and pentameters. He had neither the culture nor even the knowledge of life essential to good criticism."

If Edgar Allan Poe had not become America's first "world-author," would America have cared so very much whether his lady friends or his men friends were right in their conflicting views of him? The former would probably admit to-day that he was a dipsomaniac, and that fact would tally with the less scientific judgments of the men who saw him drunk. Did he take opium, and has it been proved that he was not a drug addict? Well, De Quincey and Coleridge were addicts, without detriment to their literary status. These researches in themselves indicate the irrelevance of Poe's enduring importance, for without the legend and the rehabilitation, what would remain? A hard-working, neurasthenic journalist, whose beautiful eyes and caustic pedantry gave him his hour of fame and opprobrium, and whose *Tales* still meet the competition of modern mystery stories. Had his habits been different, he might have profited by the success which he won with relative ease, his first prize being typical of the immediate response to his best work.

Would his fame as a world-author have been founded without Baudelaire? Admittedly not. But Baudelaire was the last person in the world to disengage Poe from the legend, being himself part of an analogous legend in France. There, however, morbidness and weakness, even vice, in the newspaper sense of the word, were known to have been compatible with considerable literary distinction. Consequently, Poe's whitewashing did not seem necessary, and Baudelaire's memory has been cleared, not of the charge that he was a wicked man, but that he was a bad poet. Nobody has yet volunteered to prove that his Jeanne Duval was white, or that his end was not due to the usual cause of general paralysis of the insane.

It was apparently inevitable that Poe should live, move, and have his literary being in his legend. This has proved more fortunate for him that if he had been exposed to posterity clothed only in his works. Whatever this lonely, frustrated man *might* have done, his potentialities are of less moment than the achievements, modest but authentic, of Hawthorne, whom he admired, and of Emerson, whom he despised. Griswold served him well when he set the ladies agog and sent Ingram in pursuit of aged dames with precious but unreliable memories. Baudelaire disappeared with him into nephitic clouds of strange perfumes, narcotic fumes, and perverse dreams. Romanticism had its last victory. Had Poe's own gods been kind, he would have edited his magazine of Pure Taste at Oquawka, Illinois, and the rest would have been silence.

Chapter Eight

WALT WHITMAN

WALT WHITMAN was the first of the literary exhibitionists whose cacophonous incongruities and general echolalia are the distinguishing marks of what is regarded as poetry in æsthetic circles to-day. He was the herald and forerunner of that ultra-violet literature, in prose and verse, which sprawls its eccentric typography and linguistic barbarisms over the pages of reviews that make "no compromise with the public taste." In his own day he was charged with immoralities which now make us smile, but we, in our turn, must charge him with a responsibility which neither his friends nor his enemies could have foreseen. They either bewailed or rejoiced at the fact that the Poet of Democracy found no audience with the plain people of his affections. How could they have seen in him the father of the Higher Illiteracy, destined to engender a horrid progeny of cénacle versifiers, who do not differ

WALT WHITMAN

from him in any excess of naïveté, save, perhaps, in his belief in the masses?

Here is a monthly magazine which modestly described itself as addressed to "those few intelligent people who, after glancing through a single copy . . . are capable of immediately recognizing that this journal remains upon the North American continent, and indeed upon this whole Americanized planet, absolutely *sui generis.*" Already, in this, the ear catches a note of bastard Whitmania which prepares the reader for such abracadabra as the following:

> I should here like to expose certain literary fragments, torn jaggedly from the hard context, fragments which, being felt out with the hammer of our intelligence, return the consistency of rock-crystal, fragments which, being thrown upon the hearth of our sympathetic understanding, betray the immense, the salt-veined, the profoundly premeditated chromatization of enkindled driftwood:
>
>> It is a far cry from the "queen full of jewels" and the beau with the muff,
>> from the gilt coach shaped like a perfume bottle,
>> to the conjunction of the Monongahela and the Allegheny,
>> and the scholastic philosophy of the wilderness
>> to combat which one must stand outside and laugh
>> since to go in is to be lost.

LITERARY BLASPHEMIES

Whitman's contempt for Tennyson, "the bard of ennui and the aristocracy," is carried a step farther by those whom he might have called his "British and American *eleves* (*sic*)"—to quote a Whitmanesque touch of mangled and unnecessary French which is still quite the thing in advanced literary circles. Thus Francis Bacon is set in the perspective of Gongorist criticism:

One may sit a long time in the mullioned and leaded and Tudor embrasures of that Lord Keeper of the Great Seal before one makes out a "beau with the muff" or a "gilt coach shaped like a perfume bottle." Nor if you do espy such, will you likely espy them in the predicament of a confrontation with "the conjunction of the Monongahela and the Allegheny." In other words, you will not generally uncover in those deeply spaded Essays wild images of the imagination, images that have been culled abroad, and encompassed here for their own sweet-smelling sakes; still less will you find such intricately juxtaposed to one another, with the odd, quizzical, poet's appetition for the showering criss-cross of quite inextricable and quite soul-dissolving overtones. Miss Marianne Moore and Sir Francis Bacon alike possess the analytical mind: Miss Marianne Moore possesses an analytical nose also, and is (as a woman should be) inclined to follow it. And her analyses, inordinately ordinate as they so victoriously are, subserve an end beyond analysis; their admirable elbows admirably *ad hoc,* their high rearings and higher boltings, their altogether porcupinity im-

WALT WHITMAN

peccable—these are just Miss Moore's private ways of delivering Miss Moore's æsthetic fact. "By their fruits ye shall know them," and by their poetical end are these wanderingly suspended periods constituted a poetical technique as legitimate as the traditionally ordained verbal complication of a Provençal sestina.

Here, then, is the barbaric yawp, modern style, with overtones of Harvard, Henry James and the Café du Dôme. The "simple, separate person" is now the cosmopolitan provincial, butchering several languages more deliberately than the master, but at liberty to print because the way has been prepared for literary illiteracy. As that opening line,

> One's-self I sing . . .

sets the teeth on edge by its ghastly pronominal clash, and the poet, for reasons best known to himself, utters "the word En-Masse," apparently in the belief that it is a synonym of crowd, so our moderns make play with barbarous discords of sense, syntax and sound:

> Having purposed that these pages might again serve merely by way of a back-stoop *éloge*.
> Did the unicorn desire, in general, advertisement of itself, did the unicorn desiderate, in particular, such thoughtless and promiscuous promulgation of what

LITERARY BLASPHEMIES

... remains a to-date quite ludicrously unsubstantiated *faiblesse*.

Now the Man of Feeling, *l'homme sensible,* will, upon reading this pertinent note, be æsthetically *bouleversé.*

Such sentences, taken at random from a modern review, reveal certain fundamental defects which will be noted in Whitman. The dominant element is obscurity. Pleonasm and tautology, the introduction of affectations aiming at literary effect, combined with the stereotyped ugliness of the commercial letter-writer—"to-date," "desiderate"—and the superfluous and usually inaccurate use of foreign words—every fault in this style has its counterpart in Whitman. That graceless, banal English of his, dog-eared from constant use in those writings which Lamb classified as *Biblia abiblia,* indicates a man without feeling for words, who would not shrink to-day from the horrible jargon of the follow-up letter of the in-reply-to-your-favor-would-say school of English composition.

The occasional felicities in his verse gain an extrinsic charm by contrast with the pedestrian quality of his prose, which becomes, at its best, competent journalese, but falls, more often than not, far below even that low level. For example

WALT WHITMAN

Of late I have two or three times occupied spells or an hour or two hours by running over with best and alertest sense, and mellowed and ripened by five years, your 1885 book (biographical and critical) about me and L. of G.—and my very deliberate and serious mind to you is that you *let it stand just as it is*—and if you have anything farther to write or print, book shape, you do so in an *additional* or further annex (of say 100 pages to its present 236 ones), leaving the present 1883 vol. intact, as it is, any verbal errors excepted and the further pages as (mainly) reference to and furthermore etc. of the *original* vol. —the text, O'C.'s letters, the appendix—every page of the 236 left as now—this is my spinal and deliberate request—the *conviction* the main thing—the details and reasons not put down.

This extract from his letters is typical in its revelation of all the faults peculiar to the type of illiterates, that is, of persons unable to use their own language in a cogent and pleasant manner— the choppy, inconsecutive style, the ugly, unnecessary abbreviations, and the obscure syntax, obviously aim at brevity and clarity, but actually achieve the opposite effect. Stylistically, this is the kind of letter which comes in each morning with the circulars and invoices and is thrown unread into the waste-basket. It bears all the earmarks of vague recollections of night-school classes in "business English." The Whitmanesque inven-

LITERARY BLASPHEMIES

tions, which merely enhance the incongruity of the whole, are such things as "best and alertest sense" and "spinal and deliberate request." Characteristic of the tawdriness of such writing are "my very deliberate and serious mind to you," and "verbal errors excepted," an obvious professional *cliché*.

With all this straining after succinctness, there is the inevitable predilection for tautologous and redundant expressions: "236 ones," "mellowed and ripened," "deliberate and serious," "write or print, book shape," "additional or further annex," "intact, as it is." When Whitman's letters are compared with those of his correspondents, such as Dowden, Tennyson, Symonds, Emerson or Rossetti, they read like the communications of a farm hand to the lord of the manor, not in tone, but in the contrast of styles. They are, in other words, the letters of an uneducated and untrained writer to men who, whatever their demerits, at least possessed a sense of dignified, comely English. Ring Lardner has deftly captured the peculiar qualities of this semi-literate English in such stories as "Some Like Them Cold." But what were the ingenuous weaknesses of the unlettered Walt are now the acquired and laborious mannerisms of his followers. To use the jargon of the schools, Whitman's tapeinosis has degenerated into cacozelon, and parenthyrson and periergia take the place of sense and poetry. He said himself:

> What to such as you, anyhow, such a poet as I?
> Therefore leave my works,
> And go lull yourself with what you can understand, and with piano tunes,
> For I lull nobody, and you will never understand me!

His own practice in accordance with this precept is too familiar to need much illustration:

> As from tall peaks the modern overlooking,
> Successive fiats absolute issuing,

or,

> Thou Mother with thy equal brood,
> Thou varied chain of different States, yet one identity only,
> A special song before I go I'd sing o'er all the rest,
> For thee the future,

or,

> Bluff'd not a bit by drain-pipe, gasometers, artificial fertilizers,

or,

> Now here and there and hence in peace, all thine, O Flag!

LITERARY BLASPHEMIES

And here and hence for thee, O Universal Muse! and
Thou for them!

or the charming "piano tune" of

The port is near, the bells I hear, the people all exulting,
While follow eyes the steady keel, the vessel grim and daring.

The "Song of the Exposition," "Salut au Monde," the "Song of the Broad-Axe," the "Song of the Redwood Tree," "Our Old Feuillage" and "A Song for Occupations" contain all the evidence that is needed to convict Whitman of being the beginning of that great deluge of Futurism, Dadaism, Ultraism and Super-realism beneath which modern literature is now submerged. From such poetic fancies as:

Maybe seeming to me what they are (as doubtless they indeed but seem) as from my present point of view, and might prove (as of course they would) nought of what they appear, or nought anyhow, from entirely changed points of view;

the transition is inevitable to lines like these:

> Those
> various sounds consistently indis-
>   tinct, like intermingled echoes
>   struck from thin glasses successively

at random—the inflection disguised;
your hair, the tails of two
    fighting-cocks head to head in
    stone-like sculptures scimitars
    re-
  peating the curve of your ears in
    reverse order: your eyes,
  flowers of ice

and
snow sown by tearing winds on the
    cordage of disabled ships; your
    raised hand
  an ambiguous signature: your
  cheeks, those rosettes of blood on
    the stone floors of French châ-
    teaux with regard to which the
    guides are so affirmative:
  your other hand

a
bundle of lances all alike, partly hid
    by emeralds from Persia
  and the fractional magnificence
  of Florentine goldwork—a collec-
    tion of half a dozen little ob-
    jects made fine
  with enamel in gray, yellow, and
    dragon-fly blue; a lemon, a

pear
and three bunches of grapes, tied

LITERARY BLASPHEMIES

    with silver; your dress, a mag-
    nificent square
    cathedral of uniform
    and at the same time, diverse ap-
      pearance—a species of vertical
      vineyard rustling in the storm
    of conventional opinion. Are
      they weapons or scalpels?
    Whetted

to
    brilliance by the hard majesty of
      that sophistication which is su-
    perior to opportunity, these
      things are rich instruments with
      which to experiment, but sur-
      gery is not tentative. Why dis-
      sect destiny with instruments
    which
    are more highly specialized than
      the tissues of destiny itself?

until finally the lowest level is reached with:

Vast cheek enclose me.

a gigantic uvula with imperceptible gesticulations threatens the tubular downward blackness occasionally from which detaching itself bumps clumsily into the throat A meticulous vulgarity:

a sodden fastidious normal explosion; a square murmur, a winsome flatulence—

WALT WHITMAN

In the soft midst of the tongue sits the Woolworth building, a serene pastile-shaped insipid kinesis of frail swooping lozenge, a ruglike sentinence whose papillæ expertly drink the docile perpendicular taste of this squirming cube of undiminished silence, supports while devouring the firm tumult of exquisitely insecure sharp algebraic music. For the first time in sorting from this vast nonchalant inward walk of volume the flat minute gallop of careful hugeness i am conjugated by the sensual mysticism of entire vertical being, i am skilfully construed by a delicately experimenting colossus whose irrefutable spiral antics involve me with the soothings of plastic hypnotism.

When such elucubrations are discussed to-day literary history repeats itself. There is the same overemphasis upon what are conceived to be indecencies as there was in Whitman's case, but the fundamental assumption of this sort of writing is hardly challenged. Contemporary criticism of "Leaves of Grass," when not engaged in ranking the author with Socrates, Confucius and Lao Tse, was chiefly taken up with references to "hexameters bubbling through sewage" and variations upon that theme. Even Swinburne could not forbear from his famous comparisons of Whitman's Eve to "a drunken apple-woman, indecently sprawling in the slush and garbage of the gutter," and his Venus to "a Hottentot wench under the influence of cantharides and adulterated rum." He was on surer ground when he said that Whitman was "a writer of something occasionally like English, and a man of something occasionally like genius." The first clause in this sentence very aptly describes the literature which nowadays invokes the name of Whitman to justify its dubious existence.

Henry James saw in "Drum Taps" the effort of "an essentially prosaic mind to lift itself by prolonged muscular strain into poetry"—a statement which is more appropriate to the Whitmaniac succession. Whitman himself showed rather the efforts of an essentially illiterate mind to lift itself by prolonged verbal gymnastics into literature. His perpetual sneers at "genteel persons, travelled, college-learned," at the "tea-drinking poet," at the "confectioners and upholsterers of verse," have been interpreted as sound patriotic reflections upon the pale imitative literature of his time by an authentic and independent American genius. They are obviously inspired by less objective reasons, for Dowden, Symonds and Emerson were certainly "used to be served by servants," and they were accustomed to "conversing without heat or vulgarity, supported on chairs, or walking through handsomely carpeted parlors, or along shelves bearing well-bound volumes." These "genteel persons" were forgiven only because they had the good sense to place "Leaves of Grass" on those shelves which Whitman unwittingly pictures as the scene of an unusual species of tight-rope performance.

The typographical eccentrics of the present time profess an analogous contempt for accurate scholarship and learning, while making a vast parade of otiose erudition which sometimes seeps over into appendices as lengthy as the work they are supposed to elucidate. The fate of the pseudo-literary is ironical. Whitman picked up all his vague rumors of ideas from Europe and fancied he was the first autochthonous poet of These States. The cosmopolitan provincials make a great show of internationalism—even their solecisms are allusive—but they remain incomprehensible outside their coterie. They become entangled in French reflexive verbs as Whitman involved himself in catalogues of things American. T. S. Eliot remains unmistakably a native son of Saint Louis, Mo., as the comic-strip, burlesque humor of "The Waste Land" testifies. Whitman, with his dream of representing "the ouvrier class" of America, remained as remote from it as that bilingual phrase.

The notes for the lectures which he once proposed to give reveal the sources of his ideas in magazine articles and popular handbooks. He dealt in the grandiose platitudes which do honor to man's capacity for self-illusion, and exercise an irresistible fascination over unfledged mystics, but which cannot be regarded as claims to the title of philosopher. Like all dealers in generalities of a sentimental but honorable kind, he offers to the faithful innumerable opportunities for diverse interpretation. Anarchists claim him as a brother, and fervid Christians have cherished him as a thirteenth Apostle. Metaphysicians find in him Hegelianism reduced to its most elementary terms, and mystics compare his teaching to that of the sacred books of the East. But the newspaper titbits he so carefully collected sufficiently explain his actual mental equipment. As a thinker he need hardly detain us. Out of all that monstrous rubble of Whitman exegesis which has piled up since he wrote the first book about himself in 1867 over the name of John Burroughs, no coherent doctrine has emerged upon which devotees can agree. Faith without works is an essential feature of the Whitman cult. Emerson best described what has baffled the commentators when he said that "Leaves of Grass" was a combination of the Bhagavad Gita and the New York *Herald*. He could smile as he said this, the faithful cannot do so. Hence their books on Whitman.

In his strenuous effort to produce poetry by and for the unlettered Whitman was caught in a dilemma of his own seeking. Declaring war on "literary" literature, he actually became himself the complete literary man, subordinating everything else to the process and result of his creative impulse. His brother's testimony as to his mode of life when at home, his refusal to form any domestic ties, his concern for the physical appearance of his books, and his complete, fanatical, at times almost selfless devotion to the fortunes of his poems, apart from himself—these are assuredly the marks of the professional man of letters, the characteristics of the self-conscious artist who believes in his mission, if nobody else does. Yet he has succeeded in deflecting criticism from his work by the ingenuous appeal of all literary gentlemen who resent objective analysis:

> Camerado, this is no book,
> Who touches this touches a man.

During his lifetime, and while the memory of direct personal contact persisted, a literature grew up about him which testifies to his power of evoking in his hearers the mood which dictated these lines. But his true literary significance must be sought in his writings and in those of his literary descendants. Whitmaniacs have followed him, but no Whitmans. His wish, "that there be no theory or school founded out of me," has been defeated. To interpose the personality of the man between the modern reader and his work is to comply with his own obvious wishes, but not with the demands of criticism. How effectively that has been done, however, many volumes of insignificant tributes and dreary, commonplace conversations with him stand as witnesses. Allowing for a characteristic lack of measure and taste in certain disciples, and for the emotional enthusiasm of others, there remains of it all merely the record of "a simple, separate person," finally engulfed in amiable garrulities, thanks to listeners of unequalled complacency.

The exuberance of Whitman's immediate friends and disciples is of less consequence than the literary succession for which they undoubtedly prepared the way. Literature was safe so long as he wore his frock coat and high hat, carried a cane, had a flower in the lapel of his coat, and wrote conventional articles and stories for the New York periodicals. The author of "Wild Frank's Return" and "Franklin Evans; or, the Inebriate" did not frequent omnibus conductors, although then his intellectual labors were such as might have appealed to them. But as soon as he put on the flannel shirt and slouch hat of self-conscious democracy he could freely associate with simple, unlettered folk who did not read him. The effect upon less ingenuous minds was disastrous. He was bound to become the centre of a cult. His imitators, with some modifications of costume, still haunt the purlieus of Greenwich Village.

The endless loquacity of his first disciples has left us in no doubt as to the hollowness of the illusion which provoked them to see in him a great thinker and teacher. Critics as skeptical as Sir Edmund Gosse admit the fascination of his personality; the attitude of the avowed enthusiasts was a foregone conclusion. It excluded all sense of critical values. Moreover, the stupidity of the attacks upon him rallied supporters who had otherwise little in common with those vague yearnings and intuitions of his which are dignified by the name of a philosophy.

If one looks over the Whitmanite group in this country, one notices that most of its members were stronger in the qualities of the heart than in those of the head. Horace Traubel, the beloved disciple, has assuredly no claim to consideration either as a poet or as a biographer—a pseudo-Whitman and a pseudo-Boswell. Dr. Bucke's excursions into the haze of a mysticism that was Transcendentalism run to seed come well up to the requirements of the so-called New Thought of to-day. Emerson's position was always the better defined for being rather uncertain, after his first salute to an undoubtedly original character. John Burroughs, having served as a convenient pseudonym for Whitman, turned to birds and nature study for his real interests. The English admirers had the enchantment of distance to aid them in their demand for something in American literature appropriately uncouth and exotic; they still show a preference for James Oliver Curwood and Zane Grey over James Branch Cabell and Sherwood Anderson. It is also overlooked, as a rule, that W. M. Rossetti coaxed them with a volume so carefully selected that even Mr. Harlan would not have demurred.

As soon, therefore, as the frock-coated, top-hatted Whitman ceased to write what the man in the street admired, he became the unread camerado of the toilers and the venerated idol of a minority of mystical and humanitarian intellectuals, mostly of an obscurity from which only Whitman's name still saves them. Peter Doyle, street-car conductor and railroad man, is reported as saying: "Yes, Walt often spoke to me of his works. I would tell him, 'I don't know what you are trying to get at!'" Yet, this poetry, "consistent with American, modern and democratic institutions" at once aroused the emotions of such "Americanos" as the British conservatives, Edward Dowden and John Addington Symonds. Moreover, the foreigners were actually closer to the mark at which Whitman aimed than the Americanos, for they could discern an obvious rawness and strangeness which fitted in with their conception of America. The American initiated, on the other hand, seem to have been attracted, not by the Americanism, but by the universality of the alleged philosophy of "Leaves of Grass."

At the same time, the American as well as the foreign champions never quite made up their minds as to the precise nature of Whitman's claim upon their attention. It has been argued simultaneously that he was a profound teacher and that he was incapable of systematic thought; that he was a great, instinctive personality unspoiled by theories, and that he was a supremely conscientious artist with a definite mission to give America a national poet, to lay the foundations of a literature wholly emancipated from European traditions. His own expositions of his work, the book which he practically wrote about himself and which John Burroughs signed, his own anonymous reviews of "Leaves of Grass," and his scattered notes all point to a conception of himself and his writings which lacked no conviction of the deliberate nature of his purpose or of the conscious importance of his literary significance. It is little wonder that, while his personal spell seemed sufficiently to explain his influence and *raison d'être,* his works demanded a more intellectual appreciation of his aim.

We may cheerfully grant, as all the evidence shows, that Whitman the man exerted most of the powers that are claimed for him. As a writer, however, he can no longer be protected by that attitude on the part of his supporters which resembles the defiance of a mother to those who would hit her "with the child in my arms." So far as the man himself need be considered, the plain facts indicate exactly the kind of person who would write as he did. His predilection for people with whom no intellectual contact was possible, followed by his acquiescence in the attentions of ardent devotees prepared to read signs of profound wisdom into his usually banal but occasionally shrewd comments; the pose of his attire; his pronounced liking for coarse foods and uncultivated society; the combination of personal cleanliness and the most sordid disorder—all these traits are characteristic of a man without refinement, education, subtlety or sensitive tastes.

Great poetry has been written in poverty, misery, and dirt. It is no reproach against Villon that he lived in the underworld, or against Verlaine that his life was passed between the gutter and the hospital. Chatterton's garret has a distinction which would not attach to the Hispano-Suiza of the modern best-seller. Poets are not measured assuredly by their wines or by the splendor of their country houses. Whitman, however, differs from the poor scholars and poets honorably known to literary history. His choice of the vulgar, the ugly, the hideous, was as deliberate as his make-up for the rôle of the Poet of Democracy. The money at his disposal would have bought him an agreeable, if simple house in a pleasant neighborhood; he chose Mickle street, the horrors of which even the imagination of the most incurable romanticists could not render picturesque. The various editions of his works, on which he expended, as we know, the utmost care, are simply dreadful examples of bad taste and bad workmanship. The edition *de luxe* of 1889 is even worse than the others, in its cheap black leather binding, with its end papers in the approved ledger style, and its pocket, making it look like an engineer's note book or a bill-collector's wallet—yet, in his seventieth year he gazed upon it with pride, and signed it beneath a superscription written in the manner of a communication from a mail-order house.

The element of premeditation in Whitman's attitude is as well proven as his lack of taste. It is neither an assumption nor a deduction, but a fact to which his own statements and actions testify. Writing his first anonymous article "Leaves of Grass" he said "very devilish to some and very divine to some will appear the poet of these new poems." Yet they are supposed to be the attempt of "a naïve, masculine, affectionate, contemplative, sensual, imperious person" to express himself in literature! Nothing would be less "naïve"—except on paper—than this self-consciousness, this excessive awareness of all the elements in his work intended to produce a shock. "A rude child of the people!" he cries, and then he proves how remote he is from that condition by complacently listing all the likes and habits which are supposed to differentiate "the unconscious teaching of a fine brute" from "the artificial teaching of a fine writer." The use of the word "unconscious" here is delicious.

How consciously he likes to picture himself as "one of the roughs, large, proud, affectionate, eating, drinking and breeding, his costume manly and free, his face sunburnt and bearded"! He can never draw attention sufficiently to his costume in the new part he has decided to play. "Never dressed in black, always dressed freely and clean in strong clothes—neck open, shirt-collar flat and round, countenance tawny transparent red, beard well-mottled with white." Such is the figure of "an American bard at last," as seen by himself, a preconceived, deliberately composed figure, as lacking in naïveté and spontaneity as the poetry, buttressed by theory, which he has to offer. The legendary Whitman, the unspoiled hierophant of democracy, the child of nature, the ingenuous seer, cannot be reconciled with these facts.

Nevertheless, it is his legend which has been accepted. This aloof and secretive man succeeded in imposing upon his contemporaries and successors the notion that he was the great Camerado, the friend and brother of all mankind, irrespective of station or sex. He could denounce a Europe which he had never seen, and his grotesque conception of it no more prevents him being regarded as the leader of a humanitarian international brotherhood than his Pan-Americanism prevents him being greeted as the poet of universal peace. In a country where slavery existed, he could fulminate against "feudal" Europe, and declare its condition to be no further advanced than that of ancient Egypt,—and yet meet no challenge save on moral grounds. He could demonstrate his ignorance and be a profound thinker—but he must not "sing the body electric," or mention the "scented herbage" of his breast, or the "aroma" of his armpits.

When he had ceased to be a worker Whitman disguised himself as one, and ceased simultaneously

LITERARY BLASPHEMIES

to write for the plain people by becoming the author of "Leaves of Grass." Although he lived chiefly in New York and Brooklyn, and delighted in the city streets, he wrote constantly about green fields and the sea. He surveyed nature from the top of a Broadway omnibus. He was quintessential he-man, as the literati conceive the species, and he attracted sedentary scholars in English libraries as inevitably as romantic sea stories arouse the enthusiasm of men whose knowledge of a sailor's life has been gleaned from the swimming-pool of the *Berengaria* or the grill-room of the *Aquitania*. He is not the poet of the American people, and when he uttered the words "democratic" and "en-masse" the only ears that listened sympathetically were those not addressed.

With the lapse of time, his false position has reached the last degree of unreality. The Americano is further than ever from "the gristle and beards, and broad breasts and space, and ruggedness, and nonchalance" which Whitman postulated. The American poet who is "no skulker or tea-drinking poet" must either have left These States or be defying the edicts of the Ku Klux and the hopes of Volstead. "The New England crowd," "the college men," whom he so despised, pay homage to him, and the best estimate of him, that of Professor Bliss Perry, has the quality which Whitman so resented, when he said: "Corson accepts me in a general way, without vehemence ... I think Corson is judicial—probably that is what ails him." To-day, as in the beginning, it is "the scholar swells" who have done most to confirm his precarious hold upon literary history.

Amongst the unjudicial, who are by no means "without vehemence," his memory is as ill-served as his purpose. The poet with a message, a gospel, who said "I don't value the poetry in what I have written so much as the teaching," is now the idol of the unhappy few to whom we owe a literature of barren æstheticism without beauty. Where two or three are gathered together to compose nightmares for compositors and to devastate whole regions of French syntax, the shade of the innocent Walt is invoked, from Zurich to Paris and from London to New York. "Out of the cradle endlessly rocking" this strange child has come, suffering from tertiary Whitmanitis, the nemesis of a literature conceived in illiteracy and born into a world more concerned, then as now, about morals than about art. If Whitman had only lacked that embryonic sense of poetry, if he had not been that "expanse of crystallisable substances waiting for the structural change that never came," as the sanest of those who met him personally expresses it, how

LITERARY BLASPHEMIES

happy he and we should be! He might have expressed himself naturally in terms of Edgar Guest and Walt Mason, and our æsthetic young men would have had no more honorable ancestor than Bunthorne.

Chapter Nine

HENRY JAMES

IF Henry James had not existed, it would be necessary to invent him in order to explain the popular conception of a "literary gent." During the last years of his life it was possible to argue in literary circles that his later and more elaborate manner corresponded to a greater profundity and subtlety of thought and characterization. While the intellectuals bemused themselves with that problem, the general public left Henry James severely alone, ignoring even the earlier novels which were not conceived in the iniquity of his mature style. Apparently the assumption among the initiated was:

If this young man expresses himself in words too deep for *me*, Why, what a very singularly deep young man this deep young man must be!

It was not until the two volumes of his letters were published that the skeptical were permitted to confirm their suspicions by the spectacle of the mouse which emerged from that mountain of words. Here, evidently, was an amiable, kindly soul, but these innumerable pages of correspondence, devoid of humor and criticism, merely justify the belief of the average philistine that all this ritual of life for art's sake is an affectation to conceal the futile activities and trivial ideas of a few self-centered intellectuals.

As his letters show, Henry James led a privileged existence from the beginning to the end of his career. His education and his opportunities were all that an intelligent young man could desire. He began to write with every circumstance in his favor, and continued to the last, sheltered and coddled, without ever knowing the pressure of those exigencies, financial or domestic, which so often hamper the artist. Wherever he went, he was at once received into the best society, using that adjective in its widest sense. He was in touch with the most prominent figures in the world of French and English letters, and was early admitted by them upon terms of equality which he appears to have been too snobbish, in certain cases, to appreciate. Others have had to struggle in poverty to gain the attention of indifferent strangers; James found his 'prentice work accepted by the kindest friends, who were in a position to be of the greatest assistance to a young writer. At no period had he to face and surmount the heartbreaking and formidable obstacles which bar the way to recognition of so many men of genius and originality. He had never to compromise any of the ideals which he professed to cherish. It has been given to few writers to pursue so independently the aims which he had set before him. In these circumstances it is natural to expect that the correspondence of such a man of letters will be a revelation of all that those privileges, combined with genius, can mean for the full development of character and personality. But there is no trace of such a revelation here. Of all the varied personalities and events with which Henry James was associated he has nothing to say that will linger in the memory. In his early youth he seems to have had some glimmerings of humor and some gift of critical observation, as when he speaks of Mrs. William Morris's "medieval toothache." In the main his accounts are no better than those of the society gossips in the fashionable periodicals. He accepted the point of view toward European society which one expects in the typical social climber of Anglomaniac proclivities. He was the diner-out and gentleman of letters, perpetually amazed, like Mr. Walter Hines Page, at his own good fortune in being allowed to breathe the refined atmosphere of the most select circles, and altogether inhibited from criticism by a sense of his own inferiority. If he did not actually count the gold plate and the number of footmen, like the American ambassador, his provincial pride swelled as he related the number of times he had been invited out to dinner. He was possessed by precisely that vulgarity from which he had proposed to escape by abandoning his own country. When he fled from America he was trying to escape from himself.

Human life had apparently no interest for him, save when it presented itself in the shape of "good society." The Civil War left no impression on him so far as is recorded, and he remained equally inaccessible to all subsequent human concerns until the Great War in 1914, and that catastrophe merely demoralized him to a state of fussy hysteria. He collapsed under its shock, but never understood what the issues were. His views were a crude echo of whatever he read in the popular patriotic newspapers. He, who could never bring himself to use the natural phraseology appropriate to common events, lapsed into the stereotyped phrases of the official spell-binders when he talked about the war. Having once spent a couple of days in Ireland—appropriately, with a Lord Lieutenant—he naturally knew exactly what to think about that country. "I don't believe much in the Irish," he writes from the Viceregal Lodge. "I can't but think they are a poor lot . . . their power to injure and annoy England (if they were to get their own parliament) would be considerably less than is assumed." Obviously, the author was more happily employed in analyzing the megrims of a duchess than in political vaticination. Yet, curiously enough, the Irish question is the only issue of national importance upon which he expressed himself in his published letters prior to the World War.

It was a more characteristic and congenial task for him to invent euphemisms in order to avoid the use of the vulgar and rather American word "typewriter." He constantly dictated his letters, and just as constantly felt it his duty to apologize for so doing, however intimate the friend to whom he was writing. But he could never do this simply and naturally. With elephantine ingenuity he devised such circumlocutions as: "Forgive my use of this fierce legibility"; "let this mechanic form and vulgar legibility notify"; "this graceless machinery"; "this impersonal mechanism." He was perpetually engaged in explaining delays in answering letters and assuring his correspondents in extravagant terms of his shame, indignation, delight, amazement, or undying love, enfolding them in elaborate phrases of the hollowest courtesy. He could never be brief, unaffected, and sincere. He even cultivated that exasperating form of facetiousness, or affectation, which consists of writing a semi-English, semi-French jargon, where no special shade of meaning requires the use of foreign words, and of course the French is highly unidiomatic.

An intelligent interest in political and social questions is not necessarily a criterion of an author's excellence, but the aloofness from life in Henry James is not compensated by any evidence of intelligent participation in the literary life of his time. Stevenson and Kipling are the only contemporary writers in whom he shows a genuine interest. The labored tone of his comment on Howells suggests that he found the latter's friendship more acceptable than his books. Of Meredith, so supremely the master of all that Henry James vainly strove to accomplish, he has nothing to say, except to complain that his letters were not worth publishing, and that *Lord Ormont* was obscure. From the author of *The Finer Grain* and the writer of the letters published by Mr. Percy Lubbock, this comment comes with a peculiar charm of its own. He does not appear to have heard of such nonentities as Bernard Shaw, Anatole France, J. M. Synge, or Remy de Gourmont. He was terrified by his association with the wicked *Yellow Book*. His relations with H. G. Wells were strange, especially in their culmination in an explosion of verbose indignation at the parody of his style in *Boon*. Anything vital, humorous, and strong was shunned by Henry James. He preferred the elaborate politeness of the most formal friendships, and felt happy only in the cloistered company of spinsters of all ages and both sexes. The atmosphere of his intimate circle is that of a tea party in an English country vicarage, with the dear rector slightly indisposed, and, consequently, much flustered whispering among the elderly virgins present.

Through all this atmosphere of spinsterhood, with its apologetic deprecations, its loving assurances, its tremors and disgusts, its feeble enthusiasms and querulous resentments, runs the plaint of an intellectual hypochondriac with a grievance. Henry James inveighed ponderously against the popular taste, and attitudinized inimitably about the sacredness of art. Yet his grievance was that his books did not sell. He had the fullest appreciation from the minority whose opinions allegedly mattered, but he envied the success of the tradesmen of fiction. Although under no economic necessity for doing so, he set himself to writing plays for money, and was the victim of the most preposterous tragi-comedy in modern literature. When his "Guy Domville" was produced by Sir George

LITERARY BLASPHEMIES

Alexander, it was a failure, but the wretched author actually came before the curtain and received the howls and hisses of the exasperated audience. This was his first and only contact with the vulgar world outside of the charmed circle of his fashionable hostesses and the incense-bearers who played up to his cult of himself. After that he returned to his mittened and velvet-gloved audience, to his Remington and its "fierce legibility," to his protestations of boundless friendship and ominously artificial delight in the receipt of some wholly unimportant book.

Only thus could he proceed unhindered with the elucubration of that famous later manner, the secret of which was so unwittingly revealed by the pious publication of his letters. What if beneath those tortuous phrases and sentences lay nothing but an obvious thought or fact, tortured into a portentous paraphrase? At school one used to amuse oneself with that sort of thing:

> Twinkle, twinkle, little star.
> How I wonder what you are. . . .

became

> Shed forth an irregular, intermittent light, diminutive, luminous heavenly body,
> How I conjecture with wonder not unmixed with surprise what you may be.

And "This is the house that Jack built" could be expanded until it was "the domiciliary edifice erected by John," and "the cow with the crumpled horn, who tossed the milkmaid all forlorn" appealed to one's schoolboy fancy as "the domesticated female of the bovine tribe who, with her curvilinear and corrugated protuberances, considerably elevated into atmospheric space the maiden of dejected mien, whose occupation consisted in extracting the nutritious lacteal beverage."
Since Henry James habitually wrote in that manner to his friends, it was inevitable that his writings intended for public consumption should show the same tendency to an exaggerated degree. The revised versions of the novels which were once unencumbered by "rich seaweeds and rigid barnacles and things," as William James expressed it, furnish the best evidence of this laborious emptiness. "He spoke, as to cheek and chin, of the joy of the matutinal steel" is the later rendering of "he was clean-shaved." "She sent every now and then a responsive glance toward her admirer" becomes "her attention addressed to her admirer, from time to time, for reciprocity, one of its blankest, though not its briefest missives."[4] "Her clear grey eyes were strikingly expressive; they were both gentle and intelligent" inspires "her wide grey eyes were like a brace of deputed and garlanded

maidens waiting with a compliment at the gate of a city." "They had not those depths of splendor —those many colored rays—which illumine the brow of famous beauties" is inflated until it reads: "they failed of that lamp-like quality and those many-colored fires that light up, as in a constant celebration of anniversaries, the fair front of the conquering type." A lady who has been described as "rather thin" later becomes "of attenuated substance," and "a foreigner to his finger tips" is "a foreigner to the last roll of his so frequently rotary *r*."

The cat is very definitely out of the bag, or, as the later James would say, "the domesticated feline has escaped from its integument of sackcloth." These quotations are not particularly obscure, and they have been quoted on occasion with admiration. Yet, do they not clearly reveal the childishness of the method whereby the author deceived the faithful? The obscurities and redundancies which were charitably supposed to have some high significance are idle logomachy and echolalia. Sentences such as "That's exactly why—if one could have done it—you'd have been to be kept ignorant and helpless," or "What was this at bottom but what had been to be arrived at?" may delight connoisseurs of oddly used auxiliaries, but the truth remains that they are deliberate and cacophonous eccentricities. Should one admire as a master of dialogue a writer who has no scruples in saying: "She surely would be sorry to interfere with the exercise of any other affection which I might have the bliss of believing you now to be free, in however so small a degree, to entertain," or "Tell my father, please, that I'm expecting Mr. Crimble, of whom I've spoken to him even if he doesn't remember, and who bicycles this afternoon ten miles over from where he's staying—with some people we don't know—to look at the pictures about which he's awfully keen."

Henry James, for all his efforts to be elaborate, rarely achieves anything other than verbose affectation. He does not attain those felicities of expression which redeem and justify the artificial manner of the great stylists. His endless straining after effect and his constant failure to achieve it are calculated to bring into disrepute all stylized and mannered writing, to encourage the superstition, dear to all schoolmasters, that "good" English must always be commonplace and obvious, as they insist when they blue-pencil every attempt at originality of expression. His fundamental inability to write well, in his maturity, can be seen in the specimens of dialogue which I have quoted, where, as in the second instance, he carefully avoids a preposition at the end, although the sprawling ugliness of the whole sentence is obviously an attempt at colloquial carelessness. But careless naturalness would surely have been preferable to what is neither carefully wrought nor convincingly natural. To quote one of his admirers, in a characteristic evasion, James's "interlocutors are merged in the monotony of their high civilization." In plain English, he cannot differentiate his characters by their speech. No wonder he objected that George Gissing overdid "the ostensible report of spoken words."

The revised and later works of Henry James afford an admirable opportunity of observing how literary legends are built up and maintained. His letters are the *reductio ad absurdum* of the man and his method. One of his friends has told us how James lay awake all night and came down to breakfast a nervous wreck merely because his friend had very soundly argued against the rewriting in his later style of *Roderick Hudson*. Biographers have sought in vain for incidents in his career which would throw any light upon his emotional life. His letters do not indicate that he ever was human, that he ever felt or expressed a natural emotion. His decision to become a British subject is the exception and, doubtless on that account, its importance has been exaggerated. Millions of people have become American citizens for reasons neither more nor less creditable or sentimental. As reflected in the eyes of the devotees, his naturalization assumes the legendary proportions of an act of vital importance to the Allied armies.

In short, the life, work, and letters of Henry James are a perfect example of the material out of which literary myths are created. As soon as he developed his later manner he, who had been unread, was no longer unhonored and unsung; he fulfilled all the requirements for an intellectual cult. The general public looked at him askance, but the *cognoscenti* wandered delightedly among his labyrinthine phrases. Had his friends been cautious enough to withhold his correspondence, we might still be arguing about the significance of his method and the beauties of his style. But only eyes beglamored by excessive reverence can be deceived by this paraphernalia of words, behind which a timid, frustrated *déraciné* sheltered his poverty of ideas and experience. Whatever he had to say will be found in those early works in which he dealt unaffectedly with the one problem that he knew at first hand, the one human situation from which he could not run away because it was his own: the American in conflict with European conventions.

If the letters of Henry James had been written by some anonymous spinster, morbidly self-conscious, and preoccupied with fussy futilities, they would, if ever published, have been made the subject of impolite merriment. But literary gents have a perverted trade-union sense and a quasi-monopoly of the channels of criticism and communication which, while rarely enabling them to combine for any useful purpose, make them conspire to conceal the emptiness of such a life as that of Henry James. Anathema has already been pronounced upon the one critic who has written a study of him which sounds the depths of the vacuum in which James lived. To have shown, however sympathetically, that this plant had no roots either in American or in European soil, was unpardonable. Transplantation does not always mean growth. Plants without roots often have the appearance of flowering, but the blossoms wither after the brief moment of their fictitious life. Those strange flowers of verbiage with which Henry James decorated the sapless sprigs of his imagination are as ephemeral and unconvincing as the potted plants which the florists design to deceive the unsuspecting for the duration of an Easter Sunday. His word-spinning represents the decline of a man of talent, not the maturity of a man of genius.

Chapter Ten

THOMAS HARDY

AS a novelist Thomas Hardy is the living link between the modern literature of our own time and the literature of the past, to which the classics, by definition, belong. His last novel, *Jude the Obscure,* was published thirty years ago, and his first acknowledged piece of prose writing dates from 1865, when he entertained the readers of that almost incredible periodical of the Victorian era, *Chamber's Journal of Popular Literature, Science and Arts,* with "How I Built Myself a House." This was the year in which *Our Mutual Friend* appeared, and it was about that time that Dickens was editing *All the Year Round,* and recommending in prefatory exhortations the *Legends and Lyrics* of Adelaide Anne Procter. A novel that was to exceed any of Hardy's in popular esteem, *Strathmore,* also introduced a new writer named Ouida, in 1865; and during the next ten years Mrs. Henry Wood, Wilkie Collins, Bulwer Lytton, Anthony Trollope, and George Eliot were the gods of the Valhalla of fiction which the architect from Dorchester had come up to London to storm. They produced the kind of fiction which soothed the leisure moments of Darwin, who had recently aroused in the intellectuals a passionate interest in geology; and so, while Gladstone and Huxley argued about the Gadarene swine, and the quaint superstitions of rationalism displaced those of Judaism in advanced circles, literature was abandoned to the plain people.

On the evidence of the few poems surviving from his first years in London, Thomas Hardy was undisturbed by the turmoil of the sixties, when what Mr. Chesterton calls "the Victorian compromise" began to break down. While still under thirty he had reached all the fundamental conclusions of his philosophy:

> If but some vengeful god would call to me
> From up the sky, and laugh: "Thou suffering thing,
> Know that thy sorrow is my ecstasy,
> That thy love's loss is my hate's profiting!"
>
> Then would I bear it, clench myself, and die,
> Steeled by the sense of ire unmerited;
> Half-eased in that a Powerfuller than I
> Had willed and meted me the tears I shed.
>
> But not so. How arrives it joy lies slain,
> And why unblooms the best hope ever sown?

THOMAS HARDY

—Crass Casualty obstructs the sun and rain,
And dicing Time for gladness casts a moan . . .

These purblind Doomsters had as readily strown
Blisses about my pilgrimage as pain.

It is hardly necessary to say that this was not the kind of poetry that editors were then disposed to regard sympathetically, nor was this Schopenhauerian conception of the universe particularly acceptable to a minority convinced that science held the key to the riddle of that universe. Thomas Hardy retired from London and decided to write fiction and, being a modest young man of thirty, with the noble company of Wilkie Collins, Charles Reade, and Mrs. Craik to inspire and dazzle him, he published his first novel, *Desperate Remedies,* anonymously in 1871, paying the sum of seventy-five pounds for the privilege. He had previously submitted the manuscript of *The Poor Man and the Lady* to Messrs. Chapman and Hall, for whom George Meredith acted as reader. Meredith rejected it, as he rejected *East Lynne,* but for diametrically opposite reasons. Hardy's defect was lack of incident and too much "talk," as to which Meredith offered advice of the kind which he himself would never have taken. *Desperate Remedies* was everything that a mid-Victorian best-seller ought to be: it contained no less than three intertwined mysteries, all held together by a love story and all solved in the last half of the book. It failed to attract any attention. The author confessed that "the principles observed in its composition are, no doubt, too exclusively those in which mystery, entanglement, surprise, and moral obliquity are depended on for exciting interest," but pointed with some pride, in 1896, to the fact that "certain characteristics which provoked much discussion in my latest story were present in my first . . . when there was no French name for them." That Hardy referred to his realistic, unsentimental attitude towards love seems to be indicated by contemporary complaints that the book was "unpleasant," and by the hope politely expressed by one reviewer in that age of innocence that the author of this outspoken work was not "an English lady."

Sad as the implications of that hope were, we must remember that George Eliot flourished in those days, and one might expect the green bay tree to give out shoots at any moment. It so happens that George Eliot's name was linked with that of Hardy when his second novel, *Under the Greenwood Tree,* appeared anonymously, and when *Far from the Madding Crowd* ran as an unsigned serial in a London magazine, it was actually attributed to the author of *Silas Marner.* The two stories have something of the quality of George

THOMAS HARDY

Sand and George Eliot in their portrayal of rural manners and the sounds and sights of rustic life, but into these pastoral scenes the tragic irony of Hardy comes with a force which lifts the Wessex novels far above the amiable romanticism and sentimentalizing of those ladies. One staunch admirer of George Eliot declares that these two are "the only novels in which the sexual passion plays no more than a normal part in the development of character. . . . Hardy's characters never pass from a lower to a higher spirituality, as George Eliot's frequently do; they are bound on the wheel of life which inexorably breaks them in its revolutions." It would certainly be difficult to find two novelists so thoroughly English and so frequently mentioned together as Thomas Hardy and George Eliot who are so radically different from each other in every respect save that of nationality.

Hardy was a youth of eighteen when *Scenes of Clerical Life* appeared; during his early manhood George Eliot established her fame and influence, and *Middlemarch* was published the same year as *Desperate Remedies*. He was, therefore, in a sense a contemporary of that typical Victorian figure, and it is in the abyss that separates them, rather than in any slight or imaginary resemblance between them, that the explanation of Hardy's vitality to-day will be found. That abyss separates him not only from George Eliot but from the entire host of writers to whose influence and example he might have succumbed—the minor novelists of the mid-nineteenth century, assuredly the most completely extinct of all writers of English fiction—as it separates him from a tradition which, as I have suggested in the chapter on Dickens, took the English novel into the nursery for the amusement of children and of adults who have never grown up. During the decade before Hardy began to write George Meredith had been offering those children *The Shaving of Shagpat, The Ordeal of Richard Feverel, Evan Harrington, Sandra Belloni, Rhoda Fleming,* and *Vittoria,* which very naturally passed unperceived by a public grovelling in *Hard Times, Little Dorrit, A Tale of Two Cities, Great Expectations,* and *Our Mutual Friend*—to mention those works of Dickens which coincided with the first ten years of Meredith's career. But Meredith was so miraculously uncontaminated by his period that he does not present the same kind of interest as the case of Hardy, who never actually emancipated himself in his novels from certain conventions of Victorian fiction, but who survives nevertheless as one belonging to our own time.

It has often been said that if Thomas Hardy had died thirty years ago his position to-day would be

THOMAS HARDY

very much what it is, in spite of his insistence during those years upon his superior claim to be a poet rather than a novelist. Strenuous efforts have been made by a few critics to recover from the first dismay created by the Napoleonic epic of *The Dynasts* and to lean so far forward in the other direction as to dismiss the Wessex novels as of little importance compared with that work and with his lyrics. Disputes on this point have something of the effect of thrusting the author, already retired from the world, so far back that he appears as remote as a classic should be. Were it not for the annual protest against the failure of the Swedish Committee to award him the Nobel Prize, Thomas Hardy would be regarded, not as an honored survivor of a departed epoch, but as a dead Victorian with a curious spark of life in his writings. And we should then be engaged in discovering the cause of that spark. As it is, the commentators are visibly impressed by the unusual situation in which they find themselves when dealing with an immortal who is still living. Immortality should not be thus complicated, for it leaves the victim suspended between the hell of academic annotation and the heaven of contemporary reviewing.

In the circumstances discussion of Thomas Hardy becomes very much what it would be were Shakespeare to be raised from the dead and to submit an occasional verse for publication. Criticism would be silent and the mildest animadversions of his most orthodox exegetists in the past would be regarded as blasphemy. Mr. George Moore discovered this when he felt called upon to discuss the defects of Hardy's style; for Hardy, unlike Moore, has not devoted these last thirty years to rewriting his early novels and suppressing those that could not be patched. Consequently, Mr. Moore could unearth the following passage from *Far from the Madding Crowd:*

> The persistent torrent from the gurgoyle's jaws directed all its vengeance into the grave. The rich tawny mould was stirred into motion, and boiled like chocolate. The water accumulated and washed deeper down, and the roar of the pool thus formed spread into the night as the head and chief among other noises of the kind created by the deluging rain. The flowers so carefully planted by Fanny's repentant lover began to move and writhe in their beds. The winter violets turned slowly upside down and became a mere mat of mud. Soon the snowdrops and other bulbs danced in the boiling mass like ingredients in a cauldron. Plants of the tufted species were loosened, rose to the surface, and floated off.

Whereupon Mr. Middleton Murry, in an essay published in a limited edition of five hundred copies, declared that Mr. Moore was an impotent writer whose books had so little appeal that they were issued in limited editions of one thousand copies, and he further declared that this attack upon Thomas Hardy's style was merely inspired by venom and envy, virtues in a young man—according to Mr. Murry—but "senile indecency" in a writer of Mr. Moore's years.

There are just two points in this debate which should interest the impartial reader. In the first place, the passage quoted does not contain such infelicities as Mr. Moore pretends. The metaphor of the torrent's vengeance is quite effective, and brown mould does look like boiling chocolate in the circumstances described. Flowers *do* writhe when caught in a rush of water, and they can be turned upside down. In the second place, "senile indecency" is not an apt description of the attitude of Mr. Moore, for his hostile interest in *Far from the Madding Crowd* is by no means a pastime of his declining years. It is just thirty-seven years ago since he first discussed this book in his *Confessions of a Young Man,* where he wrote:

I have heard that Mr. Hardy is country bred, but I should not have discovered this from his writings. They read to me like a report, yes, a report,—a conscientious, well-done report, executed by a thoroughly efficient writer sent down by one of the daily papers. Nowhere do I find selection, everything is reported, dialogues and descriptions. Take for instance the long evening talk between the farm people when Oak is seeking employment. It is not the absolute and literal transcript from nature after the manner of Henri Monier; for that it is a little too diluted with Mr. Hardy's brains, the edges are a little sharpened and pointed, I can see where the author has been at work filing; on the other hand, it is not synthesised—the magical word which reveals the past, and through which we divine the future—is not seized and set triumphantly as it is in *Silas Marner*. The descriptions do not flow out of and form part of the narrative, but are wedged in, and often awkwardly. We are invited to assist at a sheep-shearing scene, or at a harvest supper, because these scenes are not to be found in the works of George Eliot, because the reader is supposed to be interested in such things, because Mr. Hardy is anxious to show how jolly country he is.

This persistent attention to one of Thomas Hardy's lesser novels almost suggests that Mr. Moore's acquaintance with the works of the author he decries is limited, and that he is still, as Oscar Wilde said, conducting his education in public. Gallicisms, bad punctuation, and misspellings leave this passage no less open to destructive comment than the passage from Hardy. But the point of interest at this juncture is that the controversy is typical of the position of Thomas Hardy as a classic, in so far as he is scanned for defects that are passed over in contemporary writers; and his champions do not argue, but pronounce anathemas.

It is also significant that in 1888 George Moore invoked the name of George Eliot against that of Hardy, and in 1924 the juxtaposition in his mind was unaltered. He has relatively kind words for her, leading to the harshest judgment of him, although he admits that her work, "well and solidly" constructed, her prose, "rich and well balanced," were not enough "to save her from the whirling, bubbling flood of Time. . . . Lighter things have floated; hers have sunk out of sight." The same fate has not overtaken Thomas Hardy, to the evident astonishment of George Eliot's admirer, and this fact alone makes it necessary to consider Hardy in this survey of accepted reputations. He lives, therefore—to adapt the Latin tag—we must think of the reasons which have permitted him to escape oblivion.

If Hardy could be dismissed because of clumsy writing and melodramatic plots, he would long since have gone the way of Wilkie Collins, or he might survive as a source of movie scenarios. Only one, however, of his novels has been filmed, and that is the greatest. To outline the plot of certain masterpieces is often an easy way to be facetious—so easy that Mr. Moore could not resist it in his discussion of Hardy in *Conversations in Ebury Street.*

LITERARY BLASPHEMIES

But, even in his best novels, Hardy attains such heights of melodrama that in a perfectly sympathetic summary they sound ridiculous rather than impressive. He has a passion for plots, and plots that involve the maximum of incident, of coincidence, of incredible accident. One thinks of Miss Braddon as one recalls that a woman possessed of a vital secret occurs in *Desperate Remedies, A Pair of Blue Eyes, Tess of the d'Urbervilles, The Hand of Ethelberta, Under the Greenwood Tree, The Mayor of Casterbridge,* and *Two on a Tower.* The Enoch-Arden *motiv,* in its primitive or its slightly modified form, occurs in *Far from the Madding Crowd, Tess of the d'Urbervilles, Jude the Obscure,* and *Two on a Tower.* The secret wedding plays its part in *The Well-Beloved, Two on a Tower,* and *The Romantic Adventures of a Milkmaid.* The hero whose high station is obscured by poverty is found in *The Woodlanders, A Pair of Blue Eyes,* and *Waiting for Supper.* The villain as an illegitimate son works his nefarious way through *A Laodicean, Desperate Remedies,* and *Far from the Madding Crowd.* In most of these books one encounters all the other paraphernalia of melodrama, from the old-fashioned soliloquy, eavesdropping, mistaken identity, and undelivered messages to the neck-to-neck pursuit as practiced in the movies. Professor

Beach has pointed out that, in his last, his ripest, and his most intellectual novel, *Jude the Obscure,* the pattern of the story is a formula:

> Jude marries Arabella;
> Sue marries Philloson.
> Jude divorces Arabella;
> Sue is divorced by Philloson.
> Sue remarries Philloson,
> Jude remarries Arabella.

Add to this the fact that Hardy showed such an obliging attitude towards the exigencies of the custodians of the Young Person's check that a thesis has been written on the bowdlerizations to which he consented when *The Well-Beloved* was published in serial form, and another on the excisions from *Tess of the d'Urbervilles, Jude the Obscure,* and *The Mayor of Casterbridge.* The question has become a scandal even in academic circles. Thomas Hardy had none of Meredith's superb indifference to public taste and opinion. Unlike the author who shares with him the honors of the Victorian literary *débâcle,* he did not wait until the public had caught up with him; he adapted himself to the public. He approached to the attack of Victorianism by Fabian methods, for it was not until *Jude the Obscure* and *Tess of the d'Urbervilles* appeared, at the close of his activities as a novelist, that he showed the cloven hoof of ideas. It was then, as he explains in a later edition, that a bishop burned the former of these two books, "the experience," he adds, "completely curing me of further interest in novel-writing."

Midway in his career Hardy wrote one of his few essays, which is of the utmost interest because of the explanation which he gives of his own view of the novel and the implied answer to his adverse critics. The reader must not be too critical, "his author should be swallowed whole, like any other alterative pill. He should be believed in slavishly, implicitly. However profusely he may pour out his coincidences, his marvelous juxtapositions, his catastrophes, his conversions of bad people into good people, and *vice versa,* let him never be doubted for a moment. When he exhibits people going out of their way and spending their money on purpose to act consistently, or taking a great deal of trouble to move in a curious and roundabout manner when a plain straight course lies open to them; when he shows that heroes are never faithless in love, and that the unheroic always are so, there should arise a conviction that this is precisely according to personal experience." The purpose of such fiction is to enable us to dream, but Hardy admits that some turn to novels for more than food for dreaming, but he thinks we are likely, then, to mistake cleverness for intuition, to overlook a bad story because of the incidental elements, which might better have been expressed in another form. The perfect novel appeals both to the mind and the imagination, but there are few in this class. "Narrative art is neither mature in its artistic aspect, nor in its ethical or philosophical aspect; neither in form nor in substance. To me, at least, the difficulties of perfect presentation in both these kinds appear of such magnitude that the utmost which each generation can be expected to do is to add one or two strokes toward the selection and shaping of a possible ultimate perfection."

Ten years before the event he anticipated the critics of *Jude* and *Tess* by declaring that "the novels which most conduce to moral profit are likely to be among those written without a moral purpose. . . . Those . . . which impress the reader with the inevitableness of character and environment in working out destiny, whether that destiny be just or unjust, enviable or cruel, must have a sound effect, if not what is called a good effect, upon a healthy mind. . . . Of the effects of such sincere presentation on weak minds, when the courses of the characters are not exemplary, and the rewards and punishments ill adjusted to deserts, it is not our duty to consider too closely. A novel which does moral injury to a dozen imbeciles, and has bracing results upon a thousand intellects of normal vigor, can justify its existence; and probably a novel was never written by the purest-minded author for which there could not be found some moral invalid or other whom it was capable of harming."

This essay clearly shows both Hardy's predilection for novels of plot and action and the civilized intellectual standpoint from which he viewed the rights of the artist. The two points of view so rarely coincide, the fortunate purveyors of mystery and adventure stories being invariably full of moral indignation against those who cannot so profitably turn their talents to the entertainment of the mob but are obliged to write the truth that is in them.

Thomas Hardy was very conscious of that condition of puerility and insincerity into which the English novel declined during the Victorian era. In discussing Dickens I tried to show how the very success of such writers as he, utterly unaware of the shackles they were helping to rivet, established a type of English fiction and a tradition which are peculiar to the English-speaking world, at which all adult readers of other nations gaze in contemptuous wonder. Hardy's realization of the problem is apparent in his essay on "Candour in Fiction" where he says: "Conscientious fiction alone it is which can excite a reflective and abiding interest in the minds of thoughtful readers of mature age, who are weary of puerile inventions and famishing for accuracy; who consider that, in representations of the world, the passions ought to be proportioned as in the world itself. This is the interest which was excited in the minds of the Athenians by their immortal tragedies, and in the minds of Londoners at the first performance of the finer plays of three hundred years ago. They reflected life, revealed life, criticized life. Life being a physiological fact, its honest portrayal must be largely concerned with, for one thing, the relations of the sexes, and the substitution for such catastrophes as favor the false coloring best expressed by the regulation finish that 'they married and were happy ever after,' of catastrophes based upon sexual relationship as it is. To this expansion English society opposes a well-nigh insuperable bar."

His argument in explanation of this phenomenon reads a little like an indirect protest against the bowdlerization to which he submitted his serial stories and an apologia for his own conduct, for he avers that the libraries and the magazines are to blame. In both cases the readers are the younger members of the family, and so those responsible think it necessary to take precautions which they would not deem necessary for themselves. "What this amounts to is that the patrons of literature—no longer Peers with a taste—acting under the censorship of prudery, rigorously exclude from the pages they regulate subjects that have been made, by general approval of the best judges, the bases of the finest imaginative compositions since literature rose to the dignity of an art. The crash of broken commandments is as necessary an accompaniment to the catastrophe of a tragedy as the noise of drum and cymbals to a triumphal march. But the crash of broken commandments shall not be heard; or, if at all, but gently, like the roaring of Bottom—gently as any sucking dove, or as 'twere any nightingale, lest we should frighten the ladies out of their wits. More precisely, an arbitrary proclamation has gone forth that certain picked commandments of the ten shall be preserved intact—to wit, the first, third, and seventh; that the ninth shall be infringed but gingerly; the sixth only as much as necessary; and the remainder alone as much as you please, in a genteel manner."

In the face of such a public an author may ruin his editor, his publisher, and himself, or he may "belie his literary conscience, do despite to his best imaginative instincts by arranging a *dénoûment* which he knows to be indescribably unreal and meretricious, but dear to the Grundyist and subscriber. If the true artist ever weeps it is probably then, when he discovers the fearful price that he has to pay for the privilege of writing in the English language—no less a price than the complete extinction, in the mind of every mature and penetrating reader, of sympathetic belief in his personages." A true diagnosis this, but suggesting to Hardy no remedy, for he seems to ignore the fact that the circulating libraries and the magazines are simply accepting the conventions of their time. Both accept to-day what they rejected in 1890, when that essay was published, and in 1890 *Desperate Remedies* would not have been called "unpleasant," as in 1871. One of the prices paid by "the true artist" for "the privilege of writing in the English language" is that he was preceded by the phalanx of Dickens, Thackeray, George Eliot, Mrs. Gaskell, and the rest, who convinced everybody that nothing could be finer, sweeter, healthier nobler, more humorous, more tender, more sure of immortality, than a literature emasculated and divorced from all sense of reality. What was good enough for Dickens ought to be good enough for Hardy. Who was he to pretend that he was hampered within limitations which did not impede the stride of those "giants" on the hearth? Even Mr. George Moore, first of the gladiators against the circulating libraries, tries to snub him with George Eliot.

None of these people had to regret the price which Hardy had to pay, and his protest alone would suffice to mark him off as a man so far ahead of his time that we can recognize him as a contemporary. To Thomas Hardy should go the credit usually accorded to the group of almost forgotten writers who flourished for their little hour, during the well-advertised eighteen nineties, and are now forgotten outside the sale room of rare books. *Tess of the d'Urbervilles* and *Jude the Obscure* were the two great novels of the nineties, with *Esther Waters* a third of equal merit. All three were written by men who can, by no stretch of the imagination, be identified with the *Yellow Book* school, but whose revolt against Victorianism was infinitely deeper and more effective. Yet, by an irony of literary history, while George Moore sneers at Thomas Hardy, there is a ceaseless turning over of the rubble and ashes of the yellow nineties in search of imaginary treasure, and Hardy is hedged off by all the ritual usually reserved for the departed glories of English literature. His melodrama is old-fashioned, and his philosophy is now so much an accepted part of our modern point of view that, while it undoubtedly explains why he has not faded, its exposition may seem a little commonplace. An effort to evade this has been made by establishing parallels between Hardy's view of the universe and Schopenhauer's philosophy of the Will to live, with his corollary that renunciation of that Will is the only solution to the problem. Happiness is negative, as Schopenhauer once said; it consists in "the absence of pain."

Whatever the identity between their points of view (and Hardy confesses to many), it is not because of Schopenhauer that Hardy lives. His work belongs to our own time primarily because of the implied, rather than the expressed ideas that underlie his treatment of his characters. He is utterly untouched by didacticism, and even his wildest plots are relieved by touches of irony, a sardonic humor which saves them from the bathos of Dickens. When Fanny Robin, in *Far from the Madding Crowd,* is dragging her weary way to Dorchester Workhouse, her strength fails her when she is a few hundred yards from the place. She falls swooning and is aroused by a dog licking her hand. Leaning on the animal, she is helped forward to the door, where her prostrate figure is found and she is carried in. She has just enough strength to say, "There is a dog outside. Where is he gone? He helped me." "I stoned him away," said the man. It is not difficult to imagine what a lovely picture Dickens would have drawn here. The joyous barks of the noble friend of man, the bright fire gleaming, the luscious bones that would be given to him, and the general rejoicing in the workhouse over the wonderful working of Divine Providence. But how much truer Hardy's version is, and how much more moving than anything Dickens could have conceived!

It is not, however, in such slight effects as this that one should measure the distance that separated Thomas Hardy from the sentimental conventions of the second half of the nineteenth century. What set him apart was the entire absence from his mind of the assumptions, tacit and avowed, upon which the smug literature around him was based. That beautiful compromise known as "rational idealism" has been devised to the greater glory of Victorianism. Darwinism was a cruel blow, more especially as Huxley and others made it clear that one of the first, the ineluctable consequences of admitting what Ingersoll called "the mistakes of Moses" was that it became necessary to undergo the painful process of thinking for oneself, of arriving at a personal morality, independent alike of Genesis and geology. In order to soften this blow, rational idealism was evolved—a form of idealism which might be summed up by saying ideals should be heard, but not seen. George Eliot has been credited with having most effectively expounded this philosophy of rational idealism, and her "radical" ideas are contrasted with the "reactionary" ideas of Thomas Hardy.

"Humanitarian zeal in George Eliot," writes one of Hardy's critics, "is qualified by a strong recognition of the need for standards and criteria whereby to make effective the attempted reforms. As a result, although her sympathies are catholic, she never allows them to blunt her perception of the wider values involved. There is no question of obscuring sin under the name of misfortune, or of disguising wrongdoing under the sanction of necessity or expediency." Hardy, on the other hand, glorifies the liberty of the individual in all matters of conduct and behavior. "There never occurs to any of his folk the question of their relation to society at large or the possibility of duties toward any save their own individualities. It becomes, therefore, a matter of pity rather than censure when, in following the dictates of individual conscience, one or another hapless wight incurs the traditional reproach and contumely with which society, as it is at present constituted, visits offenders. The ironies which Hardy really perceives in life are nothing less than the discrepancies between action induced by the individual perception of moral relations and those traditionally accepted by social usage."

In these two quotations are summed up, I think,

all the defects of George Eliot and the whole school which she represented, and all the virtues of Thomas Hardy, which have now become social axioms. His offense was twofold. He was amoral and he was pessimistic, in the misunderstood sense of that word. He described Tess as "a pure woman" to a society which believed that chastity was the only test of purity, and he pictured her in terms which make admirers of Romola indignant:

It was a thousand pities, indeed, it was impossible even for an enemy to feel otherwise on looking at Tess as she sat there, with her flower-like mouth and large tender eyes, neither black nor blue nor grey nor violet; rather all those shades together and a hundred others, which could be seen if one looked into their irises—shade behind shade—tint beyond tint—round depths that had no bottom; an almost typical woman, but for the slight incautiousness of character inherited from her race.

It was "French" and degrading to see a woman like this:

She had stretched one arm so high above her coiled-up cable of hair that he could see its delicacy above the sunburn; her face was flushed with sleep and her eyelids hung heavy over their pupils. The brimfulness of her nature breathed from her. It was a moment when a woman's soul is more incarnate than at any other time; when the most spiritual beauty inclines to the corporeal; and sex takes the outside place in her presentation.

George Eliot's Tessa was not like Tess, nor were Hetty Sorrel and Maggie Tulliver as wicked in their waywardness as Sue Bridehead; Romola could not be described as Hardy described Eustacia, the "raw material of a goddess," her "pagan eyes full of nocturnal mysteries." Hardy has been accused of taking a "low" view of woman, that is to say, in the perversion of words to which rational idealists are prone, a view of women which accepts, admires, and understands her femininity. The quotation by J. M. Barrie of a phrase found by him in a copy of *The Return of the Native* has often been cited as illustrating the offensiveness of his attitude towards sex. "What a horrid book!" wrote some reader in the margin of the library copy. "Eustacia is a libel on noble womanhood. Oh, how I hate Thomas Hardy!" Against that it is fair to set this tribute from Miss Anne Macdonnell, the first woman to write about Hardy, away back in 1895, when only Lionel Johnson's book had appeared on the subject:

> Every woman will go straight to the point where the novelist has offended this sensitive and emphatic reader, whether she shares the sentiment or not. The offence is that Bathsheba, Fancy, Elfride, and sweet

LITERARY BLASPHEMIES

Anne Garland are fickle and wayward, they play the fool over and over again, and are totally wanting in that statuesque and goddess-like dignity that women naturally wish to have regarded as the characteristic garment of their sex. But more than that, and worse: these frail, uncertain creatures are fascinating; there is no doubt about it, each of them

> "Light and humorous in her toying,
> Oft building hopes, and soon destroying,
> Long, but sweet in the enjoying."

They play havoc with readers' hearts, and cause confusion in ideals. And it is so bad for the world to be confirmed in its already too strong opinion that attractiveness and loveableness are hardly things of the proprieties.

It is interesting to quote the whole of this comment, one of the earliest and sanest, on Thomas Hardy, for the writer has been successful in reading him, thirty years ago, with the eyes of a modern woman. Now that the possession of a vote has settled once for all the question of woman's equality with man, those who are attractive and intelligent have been quite resigned to the peculiar type of insult in which Hardy indulged in his delineation of their sex. He adopted instinctively the attitude which was to become the post-feminist attitude, and Sue in *Jude the Obscure* might have stepped out of a novel of 1927, and one, moreover, written by a woman with a vote and a college education. This picture of the women's dormitory at the Melchester Training College is typical of the situation:

> They all lay in their cubicles, their tender feminine faces upturned to the flaring gas-jets which at intervals stretched down the long dormitories, every face bearing the legend "The Weaker" upon it, as the penalty of the sex wherein they were moulded, which by no possible exertion of their willing hearts and abilities could be made strong while the inexorable laws of Nature remain what they are. They formed a pretty, suggestive, pathetic sight, of whose pathos and beauty they were themselves unconscious, and would not discover till, amid the storms and strains of after years, with their injustice, loneliness, child-bearing, and bereavement, their minds would revert to this experience as to something which had been allowed to slip past them insufficiently regarded.

The resigned and courageous, the buoyant skepticism of our contemporary conviction that "crass casualty," not reforms or laws, must govern our destiny runs through all that Thomas Hardy has written, from his first melodrama to *The Dynasts*. As he wrote in "Nature's Questioning":

> Has some vast Imbecility
> Mighty to build and blend
> But impotent to tend
> Framed us in jest, and left us now to Hazardry?

Or come we of an Automaton
Unconscious of our pains?
Or are we live remains
Of Godhead dying downwards, brain and eye now gone?

Or is it that some high plan betides,
As yet not understood,
Of Evil stormed by Good,
We the Forlorn Hope over which Achievement strides?

Thus things around. No answerer I.
Meanwhile the winds, and rains,
And Earth's old glooms and pains,
Are still the same, and Life and Death are neighbours nigh.

When it was still believed that "God is in his heaven, all is right with the world" Thomas Hardy set out to query "Nature's holy plan," not by argument but by demonstration, by showing us life's ironies, little and great. "That these impressions," as he himself said, "have been condemned as pessimistic—as if that were a wicked word—shows a curious muddle-mindedness. It must be obvious that there is a higher characteristic of philosophy than pessimism, or than meliorism, or even than the optimism of these critics—which is truth." And so it comes about that, in spite of the obsolete machinery of his stories, the characters themselves are authentic human beings, truly observed, and however he may stretch coincidence, whatever melodramatic license he may take, he rarely does violence to the truth, because his men and women are not subservient to any preconceived dogma; they are not distorted by sentimentality. Herein lies the great contrast between Thomas Hardy and his eminent Victorian contemporaries. Dickens could realistically set his stage, but the people on it were grotesques. Hardy conceives the most improbable situation or setting, and then transfigures it by the sincerity and power of his characterization. In his ironical detachment and his sense of reality this last of the Victorians was preeminently un-Victorian.

EPILOGUE

IN the distant days when Sir Hall Caine, O.B.E., had not yet fulfilled his destiny, when he was T. Hall Caine, author of a book about Dante Gabriel Rossetti, his master, he collected into a volume all the adverse criticism of Wordsworth, Southey, Coleridge, Byron, Keats, and Shelley, which had appeared in the British quarterly reviews during the first quarter of the nineteenth century. Since then several collections of this kind have been made, and every student of literature is expected to smile condescendingly when the names of Wilson, Lockhart, Jeffrey, and Gifford are mentioned. These misguided men frankly dissented from what we now regard as the accepted and only possible view of the writers concerned. We intend to be wiser—or more cautious—and our critics will see to it that the first twenty-five years of this century shall yield no such booty as may be found in these compilations, from Mr. Caine's *Cobwebs of Criticism* to Mr. Mordell's *Notorious Literary Attacks*.

Mr. Mordell's recent collection, it so happens, includes nothing later than Henley's review of the

EPILOGUE

official life of Robert Louis Stevenson, which appeared in 1901. Not only has there been a great and obvious change in the manners and method of criticism since the days of the quarterly reviewers, but even Henley's protest against the "R. L. S." legend marks a stage in the evolution of reviewing. The tendency is to risk future ridicule by an excess of amiability and credulity rather than by vigorous and independent expressions of heresy. By a fortunate coincidence, readiness to praise is a critic's surest means of attaining fame. In fact, one might compile a pretty volume under the title, "Notorious Literary Enthusiasms," and the book would be even more diverting a generation hence than Mr. Mordell's.

If it be not the supreme blasphemy, I should like to say a word in defense of the heretics of criticism. It will be admitted, I think, that the scurrility of the quarterly reviewers and the violence of their attacks on Keats, Shelley, Wordsworth, and the rest, were manifestations of political feuds and prejudices rather than positive examples of inability to understand and appreciate, or proofs of critical incompetence. The overstressing of personalities detracted considerably from the value of what Gifford and Lockhart and the others had to say. Because their judgments have, in the main, been reversed for the moment, it is commonly assumed that they proved merely their own stupidity. The corollary seems to be that one ought to beware of all such excoriations, lest a like fate befall the critic rash enough to speak his own mind frankly. Lockhart is the author of two classics of English biography, and Wilson and Jeffrey did much more for letters than earn notoriety for themselves by attacking Coleridge and Wordsworth.

From this I conclude that, while they may be charged with prejudice and even bad taste, their records establish their claim to be regarded as competent critics. Their criticism, moreover, is far too intelligent to be set aside as futile, and their errors of judgment should be attributed, not so much to their incapacity as critics as to their readiness, in certain cases, to allow political and other prepossessions to run away with good sense. The defects upon which they insisted were and are real, and it is simply our dread of literary blasphemy which prevents us from admitting in those authors who have become classics the presence of flaws which we should at once denounce in a contemporary writer—that is, if he had not yet achieved the commercial renown and success which, in the eyes of many critics, confer the same immunity from honest scrutiny as the verdict of posterity.

EPILOGUE

Nothing is more illuminating, in this connection, than the contrast between attacks colored by sheer personal prejudice and attacks clearly inspired by the refusal of the critic's intelligence to be hoodwinked by convention or deceived by spurious merit. Swinburne has survived Morley's article on "Poems and Ballads: First Series" as surely as Keats has survived Gifford's attack on "Endymion." Morley, nevertheless, was absolutely right in his main contentions, and no part of Swinburne has been more readily abandoned by his admirers to-day than that which excited the wrath of his critic in 1866. Allowing for a certain Early Victorian exaggeration in the horrifying insinuations as to the "unspeakable foulness" and the "feverish carnality" of his "libidinous song," Morley's critical instinct was sound when he ridiculed and protested against the wearisome repetition and affectation of those "quivering flanks," "splendid supple thighs," "hot sweet throats," and "all this stinging and biting, all these 'lithe lascivious regrets,' all this talk of snakes and fire, of blood and wine and brine, of perfumes and poisons and ashes."

On the other hand, Mr. Mordell's volume contains a superb specimen of the kind of criticism which is not merely wrong, but absurd because it was the work of an incompetent. Despite the fashionable habit of extolling Hawthorne, it would be easy to analyze his work, as Mr. Van Wyck Brooks has analyzed Mark Twain and Henry James, and show him to have been a truly appalling example of the wreckage strewn in the path of puritanism. That contention would be disputed, but it would lack the peculiar irritation provoked by a criticism of *The Scarlet Letter* which begins: "As yet our literature, however humble, is undefiled, and as such is just cause for national pride, nor, much as we long to see it elevated in style, would we thank the Boccaccio who should give it the classic stamp at the expense of its purity." The writer then congratulates America on having no writers "involved in the manufacture of a Brothel Library," and admonishes Hawthorne for making insinuations against the Puritans. "When a degenerate Puritan, whose Socinian conscience is but the skimmed-milk of their creamy fanaticism, allows such a conscience to curdle within him, in dyspeptic acidulation, and then belches forth derision at the sour piety of his forefathers—we snuff at him, with an honest scorn."

After this elegant flower of rhetoric, it is reassuring to hear that "we shall entirely mislead our reader if we give him to suppose that *The Scarlet Letter* is coarse in its details, or indecent in its phraseology. This very article of ours is far less

EPILOGUE

suited to ears polite than any page of the romance before us." Yet, "damsels who shrink at the reading of the Decalogue would probably luxuriate in bathing their imagination in the crystal of its delicate sensuality," and "the composition itself would suffice . . . to Ethiopize the snowiest conscience that ever sat like a swan upon that mirror of heaven, a Christian maiden's imagination." Here the writer was not an educated critic, but an obscure contributor to a church paper. The difference between this prurient drivel and the violence of Lockhart is the difference between criticism by critics and criticism by moralizing amateurs.

The spirit which prompts us to treat as blasphemous any unfavorable opinion of the immortal dead is a symptom of a change in our critical attitude which is relatively late in literary history, and which entered its culminating phase with the beginning of the new century. From poll-parroting the pedagogues who have made literature a compulsory luxury of democracy, like the possession of a vote, the plain people have learned to speak respectfully of the literary dead. The next step was inevitable: we extend the same courtesy to the living, provided, of course, they have made good. The isolated individual, with nothing to show but his originality and his independence—and perhaps a lamentable inability to make money—submits to the rigors of disinterested criticism, if he receives any notice at all. But, for the rest, we are assured that it is not the function of criticism to judge, but to convey enthusiasm.

It is constantly said—and with a misleading element of truth—that there are no writers nowadays who starve for want of an opportunity to get a hearing. Editors claim that they are eager for good manuscripts—they doubtless always have been. But if George Gissing were to rewrite *New Grub Street* to meet conditions in America to-day, would the fate of Edwin Reardon be much different? It is as difficult for a writer of his gifts and temperament to maintain his self-respect as ever. In fact, the very facility with which tenth-rate minds achieve everything that success should mean is as disastrous in its effect upon an American Reardon in 1927 as the shabby privations of Grub Street were in their effect on Gissing's hero. One may surpass Babbitt in mediocrity of ideas, yet pass as his superior by "satirizing" him, just as one may acquire profitable fame by jeering at Main Street or catering to it. The opinion of a circus acrobat or a baseball player can do more for a book than the recommendations of qualified judges. A platitude syndicated a hundredfold commands more respect and remuneration than a thousand original ideas. It takes much less time to

EPILOGUE

explain, for fifty cents a word, why one does or does not believe in twin beds, than to contract a debt with a press-clipping agency because one has insisted on issuing another work of brilliant scholarship. While one is thinking of some sparkling contribution to the debate on Classicism *versus* Romanticism, one's flapper sister has been twice divorced and is famous because of her syndicated dissertations on companionate marriage.

Such, in effect, are the results of democratizing literary education that the merchandizing of words is regarded with a seriousness wholly incompatible with the complete and widespread destruction of all literary values. In order to maintain a prestige which they have forfeited, the professional intellectuals have invented the crime of *lèse-littérature,* whereby it becomes an offense to use one's critical faculties in the presence of royalties, particularly if they exceed 10 per cent. At the same time a strenuous effort is made to enforce a system of literary ancestor worship, according to which it is blasphemy to question the divinity of the idols in the temples of letters. The person who genuflects mechanically, or in terror of the pedagogical inquisition, at the name of Milton or Shakespeare, will hardly assert his rights as a freethinker when confronted by a contemporary reputation

The academic high priests themselves evade the

LITERARY BLASPHEMIES

dilemma by the familiar process of excommunication. Ever ready to discourse about authors safely dead, they avoid pronouncing opinions about the living, save to declare that all criticism of contemporaries is valueless, as if the faculties which presumably enable them to respond to the classics were at the mercy of the calendar and did not function after a certain date. The wisdom of the infallible dogmatist is justified, at least to this extent, that the faithful are not permitted to witness the demoralizing spectacle of schism. The agnostic, however, may contemplate the dreadful consequences of the right of private judgment in the writings of those schismatics who have rashly embraced the heresy of academic modernism. Sectarians and fanatics abound among them, tinged with the evangelical unction of Little Bethel. They are as incapable of reconciling their judgments on current literature with their professions concerning the literature of the past, as they are unaware of the critical incongruity of setting *Main Street* above *Madame Bovary,* or of reciting with like fervor the names of J. M. Barrie and Shakespeare, of *Lorna Doone* and *Tom Jones.*

In short, an attitude of appreciative irreverence toward the established reputations in literature is as essential a condition of free criticism as are skepticism and heresy of honest thinking To

EPILOGUE

adapt a line of Tennyson, which is usually quoted by people who have no intention of believing it, there lives more literary faith in honest critical doubt, believe me, than in half the academic creeds.